HAUNTED
NORTHERN NEW YORK

True, Chilling Tales of Ghosts in the North Country

Cheri Revai

North Country Books
Utica, New York

HAUNTED NORTHERN NEW YORK
True, Chilling Tales of Ghosts in the North Country

ISBN 0-925168-45-9

Fourth printing 2005

Library of Congress Cataloging # BF1472.U6 R48 2002
133.1'0947—dc21

NORTH COUNTRY BOOKS
311 Turner Street
Utica, New York 13501

To my husband, Joe, and our beautiful daughters
—Michelle, Jamie, Katie, and Nicole—
and to Baby Julie, who is forever in our hearts.

Contents

Acknowledgements

You can't write a book about real people and places without help and approval from untold sources.

I'm especially grateful to the following people, in alphabetical order, for contributing in some way to the stories told in this book: Randy Besio, Joanne Deruchia, Gerina Dunwich, Nili Gold, Ronnie Guindon, Ronald and Diane Kines, Alex Krywanczyk, Gerald Langdon, Jackie LesPerance, Valerie LeValley, Gordon Little, John Michaud III, Pete and Georgi Muench, Diane and Fred Murphy, Rocco and Teresa Pepin, Doug Skopp, Tina and Greg Steiner Jr., Cindy and Greg Steiner Sr., Marjorie Thorpe, Keith Tyo, Barry and Allison Verville, and Tim Zarneke. I'm equally indebted to the following anonymous individuals: Chris H., Mark W., Tiffany, Kevin, Jessica, Karri, Andrew, Meghan, Robin, Patti, Patsy, Danny, Laurie P., Ruby, and Kimmarie B. Thank you so much for your input. You have all been very kind.

Special thanks to Chris Sharlow for allowing me to share his experiences, as well as several of his incredible photographs. They can be seen in the chapter called "Haunted Cemeteries."

The help of the many people and organizations offering leads, suggestions, permission or any other type of assistance is greatly appreciated. Queries too numerous to list were made throughout the past year, and I'd like to thank anyone who transferred my call, forwarded my e-mail, passed along my letter, or pointed me in the right direction.

Sheila Orlin, Rob Igoe, and the staff at North Country Books—thank you for believing in me and bringing this project to fruition.

Last, but by no means least, I have to thank my wonderful family for their patience, encouragement, and support over the past year. My husband Joe; our daughters Michelle, Jamie, Katie, and Nicole; our parents Tom and Jean Dishaw and Joseph "Butch" and Julia Revai; my brother Tom; and my sisters Cindy Barry and Chris Walker—I love you all.

Introduction

It all started with a conversation about ghosts at a family reunion in August 2000. My family and I had discussed the same stories many times, rehashing our experiences at every opportunity, but the hair on the back of our necks—not to mention every other square inch of our bodies—still stood on end, as if we were hearing the stories for the very first time.

One of my sisters asked me to try to research the history of a particular place to see if we could shed some light on past paranormal experiences there. As I made my way through stacks of files at the town museum, a new interest was being borne to me...local history. My love of writing, research, and the paranormal—and now local history—were all the ingredients necessary for a book on regional ghost stories. Hence, a new chapter in my life, and the first chapter of this book, was begun.

We have met ghosts, sometimes up close and personal, sometimes so obscurely as to make us question our own judgment. We have seen them, heard them, felt them, smelt them, spoken to them, and helped them. We've filmed them and recorded them, documented and categorized them, loved them and hated them. We have an abundance of evidence—photographic, audio and videotaped—thousands of credible witnesses, hundreds of motives, and volumes of eyewitness accounts throughout history and crossing all regional, spiritual and economic boundaries. Theoretically, it should easily prove beyond a reasonable doubt that ghosts do indeed exist and haunt us. *Yes, Virginia, there is a ghost.* Yet, some people are still skeptical and aren't sure what they believe.* I hope this book will help them decide.

The types of stories presented here are as varied as the ghosts who inspired them. Some prefer not to be identified, so the names have been changed, and they provide only vague information about the location. The rest include actual names and addresses. Some stories are well known around their respective communities, but most have never been told before. They may be scary, disturbing, funny or comforting. About the only thing they have in common is that they all occurred to decent folks who were kind enough to share their stories so we could better understand the spirit world that exists beyond our usual perception.

While there are many different opinions as to what constitutes a *ghost* versus what constitutes a *spirit*—even modern dictionaries refer the one to the other in their definitions—this book uses the words interchangeably to reduce the confusion.

With that in mind, let me introduce you to some of the ghosts that inhabit our very own, very haunted Northern New York.

*According to the esteemed Harris Poll, in 1998 more than one-third of people polled across the country said they believed in ghosts. An equally reliable poll by Gallup in 2000 showed that 31 percent of Americans believed in ghosts, up from 11 percent in 1978. The Gallup poll broke the number of believers down by age: 18-29 years old (44 percent), 30-49 years old (38 percent), 50-64 years old (19 percent), and 65 and older (13 percent).

Double, Double, Toil and Trouble

Fort Covington

A remarkable house sits atop a grassy knoll on a street off Route 37 in Fort Covington, and it must have one of the most extraordinary histories of any house in Franklin County. Built nearly 130 years ago during construction of the railroad, the Victorian/Art Nouveau-style mansion is thought by some to be haunted. Add to that the fact that a modern witch of the Wicca religion not only owned it, but also ran her coven and a shop called the Country Witch there as well, and you can imagine the stories that have been brewing in this straitlaced little North Country community!

First, there is the story of a beautiful, but feeble-minded, young lady who was reputedly locked in one of the attic's tiny rooms in the early 1900s by her sister, an eccentric spinster left to raise her siblings. Not knowing any better, families at that time sometimes banished their mentally retarded kin to basements, closets, and attics to keep them out of the public eye and safe from harming themselves and others. The caged and delirious woman banged and clawed at the doors and walls until her hands and fingertips were raw, leaving a mosaic of bloody handprints throughout as a testament of her futile attempts to free herself from her makeshift cell. After her untimely demise, several coats of light green paint were applied to the walls and door in an effort to conceal the blood. But no amount of paint could hide the lingering invisible evidence of her horrific plight; the pounding that could be heard in the attic long after her death and the cold spot which stubbornly persisted in one area of the tiny room, perhaps the very spot where her tormented spirit finally escaped its physical confines.

Photo by Gerina Dunwich
Attic window where an insane woman was confined until her death.

Another legend associated with the house has the spirit of an old hag wandering restlessly about. Her ghostly presence was said to occupy the bedrooms, basement, and carriage house of the mansion. She was believed to have been a witch who lived and died in the house many years ago, and though she was a probably a harmless witch—she was still a witch, nonetheless. At the time of her passing, witches, like wolves, were still stigmatized by an ill-informed society that harbored centuries-old misconceptions about them. Hence, the unsurprising rumors of the "wicked" witch that haunted the house on the hill.

The carriage house was the first structure built on the property, and it was used to shelter several carriages in the early days, then more modern vehicles as time went by. Today it's more likened to a barn or storage shed. Inside of the carriage house was a hidden trap door with a ladder leading down to an underground tunnel. The kind lady who described it to me said that she had been down there once when the school superintendent who owned it at the time invited her entire class to the house. It proved to be her favorite part of the grounds. She believes the tunnel led to the Salmon River, although the students didn't traverse the length of it for safety reasons. It's believed, however, that slaves escaping the country via the Underground Railroad system in the late 1800s would take that tunnel to the Salmon River, and then continue by boat to the St. Lawrence River where they were able to cross to Canada and to their freedom.

In 1994, Gerina Dunwich, a modern-day witch and renowned author of more than twenty of today's best-selling books on witchcraft, felt called to the North Country, and specifically to this house, with its colorful history. Getting in the spirit (excuse the pun) of the

Gerina Dunwich

legends she had heard about her new home, she turned a part of the house into an antique and New Age shop called The Country Witch. In 1996 she established a witches' coven called Mandragora and presided as the High Priestess. She also created the nation-wide Pagan Poets Society and a local group called North Country Wicca.

The townspeople became increasingly concerned that the "strange outsiders" from California were practicing black magic and performing satanic rituals and animal sacrifices at the old mansion. But Wicca is a Pagan religion based on respect for earth and nature. In fact, the main precept of the Wiccan Rede, a poem that serves as a guideline for Wiccans to live by, is to "Harm None," as you can see from the following stanzas.

Bide within the Law you must,
in perfect Love and perfect Trust.
Live you must and let to live,
fairly take and fairly give.

Light of eye and soft of touch,
speak you little, listen much.
Honor the Old Ones, in deed and name,
Let love and light be our guide again.

Be true in love, this you must do,
unless your love is false to you.
These eight words the Rede fulfill:
"An Ye Harm None, Do What Ye Will."

The last line means you can do as you please, as long as it harms nobody—not a person, animal, the earth, or the self. The religion preaches harmony with all life forms—similar to the well-accepted Native American spirituality and philosophy. Hardly the work of devil worshipers, but that point was mute to the unaware, and the rumors became increasingly unkind.

About that time, the great Ice Storm of '98 struck northern New York, and damage to the old home was quite extensive, as it was to many structures throughout the North Country. It was the final insult and an omen to Ms. Dunwich that it was time to put the house up for sale and move back to a more accepting and hospitable California. There she continues her prolific writing and speaking career today. She says, of her former house:

"As far as my own personal experiences with the ghosts there, I can tell you that I—as well as family members and friends—had quite a few!

"The first night I spent in that house, I had a nightmare that a door appeared on the wall in front of my bed. It opened and I saw a faceless man dressed in black standing there. Without uttering a word, he gestured for me to take his hand and follow him to whatever waited on the other side of the door. I felt if I did I would meet my death, and I screamed, 'No!' He instantly vanished, and the door slammed shut. At that precise moment I woke up. My lover, who had been sleeping next to me, also woke up. I thought I might have awakened him by screaming in my sleep and began to apologize. He said that it was a loud noise (not a scream) that woke him up and was surprised that I didn't hear it also. I asked him to describe the noise and, when he said it sounded like the slamming of a door, chills raced up and down my spine.

"About nine months later (shortly before Halloween), a friend from Boston came out for a visit and slept in that room. For three nights in a row, she had nightmares that a man in black was holding her down on the bed while a woman wearing a Victorian-styled dress tried to choke her to death. We performed a ritual to bless the room and put the spirits that haunted it to rest. It seemed to work because my friend experienced no nightmares for the remainder of her stay. However, on Halloween night we had gone to the graveyard on Route 37, placed a candle on a previous resident's gravestone and tried to contact her spirit to learn if she was the one who was haunting the house and why. The candle blew out and some unseen force picked up a stone and hurled it at our car, which was parked nearby. We quickly decided that it was time to leave!

"Some of the ghostly happenings we experienced included lights going on and off by themselves, our bedcovers being slowly pulled down to the foot of the bed, a vacuum cleaner turning itself on, strange unexplainable noises, and window shades in the dining room that would suddenly go up for no apparent reason. We would often find strange bats flying around in the house at night, even though all the doors and windows were locked up tight. We had one cat who seemed to be very uncomfortable whenever she entered the dining room. One night we found her in there, growling at some invisible thing. Suddenly, the crystal chandelier began to sway to and fro, and, with her fur standing on end, the cat ran from the room and hid down in the cellar. It took several days to get her to come back upstairs.

"Although paranormal events happened throughout the house, most of it seemed to be centered in the attic. It was not unusual for us to hear strange creaks and banging coming from the attic at night. I, as well as others in my coven, felt cold spots in a small room in the attic where a mentally disturbed woman was rumored to have been kept locked away nearly a half century before we purchased the property. One night, after we had conducted an uneventful séance in the attic and were descending the stairs, we were showered with at least a dozen old nails that seemed to materialize out of nowhere.

"One time while I was in Florida and my mother was staying alone at the house in Fort Covington, she heard a sound in the middle of the night that she described as either a "bowling ball or a head" rolling down the steps leading up to the attic. When she went to investigate it the following morning, there was nothing to be found. She also told me that she saw a glowing ball of light moving through the basement one afternoon and she felt like she was being watched."

The next, and current, owners saw the opportunity to restore the home to its original elegance and purchased it from Ms. Dunwich. The beautifully restored structure is now used as a peaceful, attractive home for the developmentally disabled—what a wonderfully ironic turn of events, considering the home's most famous legend of the woman in the attic. Her spirit must feel appeased, for the house currently is void of any spirit activity.

The property is private and should not be disturbed by the uninvited.

DocRoc's Z-Bar

Malone

DocRoc's Z-Bar

In the late 1800s and early 1900s, it was a thriving bordello, a bar, and a gambler's den. Ladies of the night awaited train travelers passing through the small rural community at Malone Junction on their way to Montreal. The Madame who owned the place was quite the entrepreneur—she paraded through the streets in a wagon led by two white horses and met the train at its stop so that she could lead potential clientele straight to the door of her bordello. It was an excellent marketing tactic, actually, and it ensured a steady income. Not all of the money that exchanged hands was between the prostitutes and their customers, however. On the third floor, gamblers played their games of high-stakes Poker. Some won, some lost. One unfortunate soul became the likely anonymous star of this story.

Rocco Pepin bought the building—one of the village's oldest—in 1986. It is located in the center of downtown Malone, on the right side of the road at 57 Catherine Street. In the fifteen years that he has owned it, Rocco and his wife Teresa have clearly put a lot of heart and soul into the establishment they called "DocRoc's Z-Bar." Nostalgic prints, posters and magazine ads that he painstakingly collected over the years adorn the walls of the bar. Much of the original structure and layout of the building remains in tact, making it easy for Rocco to provide the grand tour, complete with history in all its scandalous detail. But soon all of that will change when Rocco sells his beloved bar and the new owner levels the structure to make way for an adjacent store's expansion.

The Pepins recall many unexplained incidents that lend credence to the rumors they had heard of a ghost haunting their bar. When they first bought the place, there was an ornamental carved coconut head balancing precariously in an old, unused chimney flue near the stairway. For five years, the coconut head never tumbled or tipped, even with all the usual noise and activity of a nightclub. Then one day, Rocco moved the coconut head to a shelf in the poolroom and placed an old lantern he had brought from Connecticut in its place. Shortly afterward, there was a loud crash, and Teresa and Rocco met each other running to see what the commotion was. The lantern had somehow removed itself from the chimney and placed itself upright and unscathed in the exact spot it had previously sat, under the nearby countertop. That was strange enough. But even more bewildering was when Rocco's sister put a vase of gaudy flowers in the same chimney flue shortly after that, then walked away for a few minutes. When she returned the flowers were all laid out in a nice, neat row on the floor near the chimney.

Another mystery occurred at the bar one night after a band from Ottawa had finished performing and the employees and patrons had left. Teresa remained alone at the bar to clean up. When she was done, she was unable to find the bar keys anywhere. She searched the countertop of the bar and the whole area thoroughly, but with no success. The next day, she asked Rocco if he had found the keys. He told her they were right in plain sight on top of the bar that morning when he got there—in the same place she had gone over with a fine-toothed comb the night before. He also told her that while he was counting receipts in the back of the building, the dance floor lights were going on and off by themselves, prompting him to move to another spot to finish his task.

The karaoke machine sometimes stopped right in the middle of a song—delighting the crowd but embarrassing the singer—even though the wiring in the building was new and the equipment was in good working condition. Their ghost certainly had a sense of humor and mischief. Another time when a customer brought his dog into the bar and set up food and water bowls in the back room, he returned a little later to find both bowls missing. They've never been found.

The Pepins believe they have just one ghost and feel that he is harmless. Apparently, a man died from injuries sustained when he was shoved down three flights of stairs in the bar after a night of gambling in the early 1900s. He landed at the bottom, right next to the door to the kitchen where employees have felt a transitory cold spot. A doorman once told the Pepins that he often saw shadows going past the kitchen door at the same moment that cold rushes of air could be felt.

Whether the man's spirit continues to haunt the new building going up on the property or disappears into the dust of the old building's demolition, nobody knows. But it's a certainty that he will not soon be forgotten.

The Keeper of the Brook

North Lawrence

I suspect ghosts have as many reasons for hanging around a place as we, the living, do. They may have the proverbial "unfinished business," such as avenging their death or leading a loved one to important documents. They may be lost and confused—unsure of where they are or how they got there—especially if the death was instantaneous and unexpected. Their image may be caught in a time loop, replaying a particularly defining moment in their earthly existence over and over again for all of eternity. Some ghosts just like to scare us, remaining as wicked in death as they were in life. Then there are those that stick around to watch over things, making sure their loved ones or properties are well cared for before they feel comfortable moving on. They have an affinity for the place or the people who reside there, and there's no place they'd rather be, even though they could. Sloan falls into this last category.

Sloan is a spirit who has been called "Guardian of the Land" and "Keeper of the Brook" on a peaceful piece of property in the small town of North Lawrence. During a channeling session more than ten years ago, it was revealed to the current owners of the property that Sloan had kept the land from becoming occupied until someone meeting his unique standards could purchase it. He and his constant traveling companion, a spirit bear, would scare off anyone but the intended caretakers of the property in the meantime. Their means of frightening people were mild by any ghost's standards, but effective nonetheless. In this way, Sloan bided his time until the right folks came along.

According to the 'chosen' ones,

> "In the spring of 1990, we applied with a few local realtors and oriented our search for land to a small farm that would provide secure housing, good pastures, and good woodlots. So began our journey to our home and to a friend we have grown to know as the 'Keeper of the Brook.' Over several months, we looked at two places in the town of Brasher. Each was not quite what we were searching for—fields too low, structurally unsound bridges leading to the buildings, and just not a good feeling about the farms."

After looking at several more places that still didn't feel like home to them, they gave up on realtors and wondered what they would do next. Not long after, the current owner explained,

> "My wife and a friend were horseback riding down a trail to the south that crossed over a brook and onto the Morgan Road. The high school kids referred to this as the 'Boston Cow Path,' and years ago it was quite a party spot on hot summer nights. Our friend knew we were searching for land, and she and my wife started talking about what a good spot the abandoned fields would make for a couple who wanted to become part of the land and protect the area. She had grown up with the family who owned the land when it was an active dairy farm and offered to contact them to see if they would be interested in parting with a parcel on the south side of the road."

As fate would have it, the land was indeed being sold in various pieces. The parcel the couple was interested in consisted of fifty-five acres, and while the previous owner could have accepted more from another interested party from downstate, he felt compelled to sell it to this couple because they seemed perfect for the land. Recalling that time, the current owner said,

"Perhaps one of the most attractive features was the brook. It flowed all year long, and on top of an old cut bank that rose fifteen feet above the channel was the perfect spot for a house. It left a gentle grade to the brook that would make a beautiful and very private yard. We would come to learn that the brook was the key to our location. The name of the brook, interestingly, was my wife's maiden name, and according to the USGS topo sheets, every piece of property we had looked at was on this brook, or just down from where it entered another stream."

In the fall of 1990, the couple began clearing the area for the house and yard. They cleared a campsite by the brook and set up a fire pit and tent. They would spend several nights camping out on their new land, and they would be introduced to Sloan and his bear.

"Once in a while, during the first night there, we could hear what sounded like footsteps in the brook, as if someone was walking in front of us, but there was never anyone there. Our dogs heard the same sounds and would sniff around but come back unconcerned and curl up with us once more. On one of the campouts, early in the evening, we had some friends there for the fire. Again, we heard footsteps in the brook, only this time a growling noise just inside the woods followed. The noise was distinctly a bear, snarling and pawing, but there was no sound of it approaching in the dry leaves. It just seemed to appear with no warning. The dogs jumped up and stared into the woods but made no attempt to go over. The growling did not seem dangerous to my wife and I, and it stopped as quietly as it had begun. Then, with the fading sound of the footsteps in the brook, all was quiet once more. We searched with flashlights but found no trace or sign of the bear in the leaves or the banks of the brook. Our friends were quite spooked and decided they'd had enough and went home. The footsteps have occurred many times since then, but the encounter with the bear was the first and last."

While the land and the brook have been very good to their family over the years, offering protection and provisions, several friends who grew up nearby have told them that it was always believed to be haunted. They remember that, as youngsters playing by the brook, they once heard footsteps and saw soft shimmering lights coming towards them, promptly scaring them off the property.

The "Keeper of the Brook" was defending his territory, warding off unworthy intruders—waiting until he could pass the torch to the new guardians of his land.

The Franklin County Poorhouse

Malone

Photo by author

Franklin County Poorhouse as it appears today.

On a windy night, it's easy to find a scientific explanation for the chorus of eerie moans that emanate from within the many walls and corridors of the old abandoned structure. Windows are broken, and some of the doors are slightly ajar, providing ample opportunities for the wind to slip through the cracks and create a mournful symphony.

It's harder to explain the cold gusts of air that brush past trespassers on calm days as they stand amid the ruins deep within the building, or flashlight and camera batteries that go dead at the moment those cold gusts are felt.

Maybe it isn't such a far stretch of the imagination to consider that some of the haunting moans and their accompanying chills might come, not from the wind, but from the poor souls known to have lived and died in the home in the past century and a half, starving for attention now, as they surely must have then. The conditions the earliest occupants of the poorhouses endured would be enough to make anyone moan for an eternity.

In 1824 a law was passed to house, in a more economical manner, those in a community who could not support themselves and were a burden on their families and their communities. The "Overseer of the Poor," an elected official, would review an individual's request, and if accepted, he would provide them with food, fuel, clothing and occasionally medical treatment. Tax money was used for this purpose, which was known in those days as "outdoor relief," similar to today's welfare. If the person was likely to need long-term assistance, was completely unable to care for him or herself, or was caught begging in public, the Overseer of the Poor could commit them to the county poorhouse. In this way, poorhouses soon became melting pots of needful individuals that included paupers and beggars, orphans, the mentally and physically handicapped and the destitute elderly.

Many years later in the early twentieth century, the creation of Worker's Compensation, unemployment benefits, and Social Security lessened the need for poorhouses. Laws were passed prohibiting children from residing in poorhouses and requiring residents to be transferred to facilities that were deemed more appropriate for their specific needs, such as nursing homes, orphanages, mental hospitals, and general hospitals. The poorhouse was destined for extinction.

The Franklin County Poorhouse, located about two miles outside of Malone on Route 11B, started out as a two-story farmhouse in the early 1800s. By 1857 it had become necessary to expand the building. According to a document reporting the condition of the home, as required by the State (*State of New York, No. 8. in Senate, Jan. 9, 1857, Report*):

This house . . . is illy fitted for its present uses.

The basements of the building are occupied for domestic purposes only. In the house are eighteen rooms or wards, well warmed by stoves, but without ventilation. From one to eight paupers are placed in a single room.

The number of inmates was thirty-eight, fifteen males and twenty-three females. Of these twenty-eight are foreign, ten native born; nine are under sixteen years of age. The sexes are separated at night, but mingle together during the day. The average number of inmates is forty-eight, supported by an expense of thirty-one cents per week each, exclusive of the products of the farm. The paupers are employed, the men on the farm, the women about the house. The food of the pauper is of a plain and wholesome quality. The house is supplied with Bibles, but there is no regular religious instruction. A teacher of the common English branches was employed in the house for three months during last winter, but the children usually attend the district school.

A physician is employed by the year at $28, and comes only when called. There are no facilities for bathing. One birth and two deaths have occurred during the last year (1857). No contagious diseases have raged.

Of the inmates, seven are lunatics, three males and four females, all paupers, none are reported improved or cured. But one is constantly confined, and he in a cell. They are restrained by confinement, and sometimes handcuffs, shackles, and the straight jacket are used. Two have been admitted within the year. They receive no medical or other attendance, nor does the house permit classification. The superintendents usually discharge the insane; sometimes the power is exercised by the keeper. Two of the paupers are blind, four idiots—two male, two female.

The keeper reports nine-tenths of the paupers as here by reason of intemperance and its effects.

There is here a poor cripple, almost idiotic, whose limbs are drawn up and under him in strange contortions, and his tongue paralyzed by the disease. He can wear no garments but a loose shirt.

The unnatural parents were committed to prison, and the child sent to this house.

The hospital department of the house is wretched, and the nursing and medical attendance inadequate.

With the extinction of the poorhouse in American history, the Franklin County facility became more specialized, serving only the developmentally handicapped for a good portion of the twentieth century. Living conditions were then greatly improved, and the residents received the care they required. But it was too little, too late for the prior tenants, who succumbed alone in their anguish, as despondent as they had been the day they first arrived at the poorhouse. Maybe they are still there, too confused to escape their self-imposed confinement.

Gerald Langdon, now the owner of the property, doesn't believe his old building is haunted and, in fact, chuckles at the thought of it. But he enjoys hearing the stories as much as anyone. Whether the structure, which grew over the years to one hundred one rooms and four floors, is indeed haunted or not, the history of its poorhouse days is indisputable and as disturbing as any haunted house tale associated with it.

The property is private and should not be trespassed upon.

Tau Epsilon Phi Fraternity House

Potsdam

Tau Epsilon Phi fraternity house.

A salesman is found brutally murdered in a guest room that was locked from both the inside and out. Footprints of the likely killer are seen in the snow leading from the house to the garage, but no footprints are found coming out. It remains an unsolved mystery. A woman hangs herself in her wedding gown the night before an arranged marriage. A domestic laborer is gravely wounded in a tunnel collapse beneath Potsdam and is granted his dying wish to be treated as a rich man and allowed to die in his master's bedroom suite. Besides the bizarre nature of their stories, all of the above people have one thing in common—they now haunt the very place of their demise, the Tau Epsilon Phi (TEP) fraternity house in Potsdam.

The mansion known as the "TEP house" towers proudly over the valleys and fields of Sissonville Road. Sitting on top of the second hill, the hundred-year-old white building has but one visible neighbor, a contracting company directly across the road. The home has aged well, and you can easily get lost in a daydream staring up at its haunting beauty, wondering if the sordid stories you've heard about it could possibly be true.

A settler from Vermont purchased the property in 1811. For many years, his family ran a farm on the land. Then in 1886 it was sold to a Potsdam schoolteacher, the son of a prominent Potsdam businessman, who had turned his sights to agriculture. He developed the property into a prosperous working farm, with a herd of highly desirable Jersey cows that produced milk and fine Jersey butter. He eventually purchased over four hundred acres of land surrounding the farm, tore down the original farmhouse, and built the majestic house that remains to this day in its place. There, he and his descendants resided for more than seven decades until most of the family had passed on or moved away. The property changed hands several times, the last being in 1968, when the brothers of Tau Epsilon Phi purchased it.

The brothers enjoy sharing the stories they have heard or experienced in their fraternity house over the years. And, while one can speculate as to who the ghostly star of each story is—or was—I was unable to find any evidence to prove or disprove the various opinions. I do think that each and every story adds another piece to some massive puzzle, but the pieces are few and far between, and the cover to the box is missing! So we're left without the full picture, wondering whom, what, and when; but at least we know *where*.

Nili Gold, a fraternity brother who pledged in 1996 and is very knowledgeable about the stories associated with the house, offered to give me the grand tour, complete with tales. I was not disappointed, and neither was my ten-year-old daughter, Katie, who accompanies me on all of my book-related adventures and aspires to be a writer herself.

The kitchen, dining room, living rooms, and TV room are laid out in a sprawling, airy fashion on the first floor. The house still has the original woodwork that stands out as you start up the staircase to the second floor. There are fourteen bedrooms on the second and third floors. Most of the bedrooms have been given names that say something either about the history of the room itself or the person who currently sleeps there.

First stop on the second floor was the "Salesman's Suite." This room was built as a guest room with locks on both sides of the door, thus ensuring that the guest didn't come out while everyone was asleep and rob the well-to-do residents. A traveling salesman once arrived very late and was offered the room named in his honor to settle in for the night. The next morning, he was found dead. Suicide was ruled out. The door to his room had been locked on both sides and had not been tampered with. The police were called, and they found that all of the windows were closed and secured. The window overlooking the parking lot clearly revealed fresh footprints in the snow to the shed, but no footprints coming out of the shed. The mystery has never been solved.

The "Frying Pan Room" got its name because of the heat generated by the huge bay window facing east that garners the morning sun. As you walk in, you see a wall with bookshelves to the left, the large bay window directly ahead, and another wall and closet to your right. The story goes that a young lady was once locked in this room when she threatened to run away if she were forced to marry an uncle—to keep the family wealth within the family—in an arranged marriage. To ensure that the marriage occurred as planned, it is said that her selfish family confined her to her room until the wedding morning, when she would be released to fulfill her destiny. However, on the eve of her wedding, she donned her bridal gown, tied a rope around the bulb socket in the closet, and hung herself. She was found the next morning hanging behind the closet door. You can literally feel an almost suffocating presence near the door today. One of the fraternity brothers' dogs, Kylie, stands and barks at the door for hours, and the door refuses to stay securely closed. The ghost of the bride has been seen in other areas of the house and is called the "White Lady."

One night some of the brothers playfully drew a large pentagram (witchcraft symbol) on the third floor with chalk. They were duly rewarded with noises strange enough to wipe the smiles right off their faces. They made haste to the safety and security of the Frying Pan Room on the floor below. But, once there, they again heard loud noises and watched in disbelief as a wall hanging of Led Zeppelin puffed out from the wall like a horizontal parachute. And if that weren't enough, books on the bookshelves started popping randomly out, like some cheap Hollywood ghost flick. Needless to say, the brothers haven't dabbled recklessly in witchcraft since.

The "Chancellor's Suite" gets its name because the leader of the house (known as the Chancellor) generally chooses to reside there. It was the master bedroom of one of the prominent families that lived there.

Legend has it that there were underground tunnels built between houses in town also belonging to the family, possibly as part of the Underground Railroad, or maybe just for the family's own convenience. A kindly black man named Otis, who may have been either a slave using the Underground Railroad or a domestic servant, was in one such tunnel when it collapsed. The couple that owned the house at the time knew the man would not make it and asked if there was anything they could do for him. He said he wanted to live as a rich man for his last days, so they gave up their master bedroom and waited on him until he passed away one week later. Before he died, he told them that, to show his appreciation, he'd stick around in spirit to protect them. True to his word, he is the most active ghost in the house and gets blamed for a myriad of harmless, silly things that occur. When your arms are full, doors seem to open automatically. The TV mysteriously changes channels, and video cassettes literally fly across the room, if Otis doesn't like what's playing. The sound of someone playing pool in the basement has been heard by a few of the brothers, yet when they went to the basement to see who was down there, the lights were off, nobody was around, but the balls were rolling across the table.

A playful ghost recently visited the ever-inviting "Come-In" room on the third floor. An ex-chancellor of the frat house was sleeping in bed when he felt someone pushing on him to wake him up. He rolled over, trying to ignore what he thought was a brother, but it happened again. This time when he rolled over, he saw that it was a small boy. The boy leaned over him and said, "Do you want to play?" By the time the poor guy had wiped the sleep from his eyes, the apparition was gone.

The "Tent Room" gets its name because of the sloped walls and small area. Children who sound like they are playing or laughing are often heard in this room, especially by girlfriends of the brothers. One unlucky brother was sleeping in this room in the early Nineties when he woke to find the "White Lady" standing at the end of his bed, partially through the wall, because a solid physical form could not possibly stand in that small spot. She grimly told him the date on which he would die. Terrified, he packed up and left immediately and has never been back. He graduated from Clarkson in 1993 and told the brothers that he would leave specific instructions in his will to give the date that the White Lady told him to anyone who was living in the house at the time of his death, but only if the date did indeed turn out to be accurate. He did not, however, share that date with the brothers. Nobody has heard from him since, which is good news, I guess.

While reading in his bedroom during winter break one year, a brother clearly heard voices that seemed to emanate from the "Come-In." He found the room locked, just as the occupant had left it, so he tried to ignore it. When the sound of someone talking continued, however, he called another brother, who reinforced his first inclination to ignore it. It was impossible, especially since he was alone in the house. He called his mother who sensibly told him to call the police. The police brought in a dog that sniffed through the entire house, but since the door to the room where the voices were heard was locked, and the talking had since stopped, they didn't force an entry. Yet, when the room's occupant returned from break, he found the door to his room opened! Neither the police nor the lone brother in the house at the time had unlocked it.

Another story that cannot be supported by any historical data says that there were children with varying degrees of birth defects, due to intermarrying between relatives who didn't want to share the family's wealth by marrying outsiders; and the children were neglected and left to wander through the tunnels and crawl spaces that ring the entire house and basement. In reality, public records do show that at least two children died at a very young age while living there; however, their deaths were due to natural causes, and they belonged to a well-known, respectable family. When they died, they were allegedly buried in the family's own graveyard behind the house, to avoid public scrutiny and conjecture. Could it be their voices heard laughing and playing in the Tent Room? A tantalizing story if true, but highly unlikely based on my research.

While the rumors of tunnels on the property are widely accepted today, they cannot be confirmed because of an old court ruling stating that there can be no excavation or exploration of said tunnels. However, certain incidents seem to support the existence of the tunnels and graveyard. The brothers of the house brought in a psychic once who went through the house offering information that agreed with what they had experienced and heard about. She then came to a solid concrete wall in the basement and said, "There's a room here." The brothers wasted no time breaking through the wall with sledgehammers and did find a very small room. Perhaps the room is an entry point to the tunnels, though no further excavation has been done to confirm that suspicion. Or perhaps it's just a large empty cistern, but why block it off with a cement wall?

The annex area directly behind the house is where the brothers believe the family graveyard was, before being turned into servants' quarters. They didn't dig and pour a foundation over the area, because there are rules and regulations to conform to if you actually unearth any human remains. So they built "The Outback" up on posts to provide space for six more bedrooms, bringing the total number of bedrooms in their house to twenty, enough to sleep forty-four brothers; although, it has accommodated more. The Outback has now fallen into a dilapidated state and will soon be torn down.

The Spirit of Olivia

Nicholville

LesPerance home as it appears today.

The blaring headline read in large print "Girl Murdered, Lover Sought." Big news for a small-town newspaper in Potsdam, New York, in 1901. Big news still, for a small-town newspaper one hundred years later. On March 25 of that year, Olivia Goodnow, a nineteen-year-old servant girl, was found dead at the home of her employers, Mr. and Mrs. Charles Brush, who Olivia lived with on a large ancestral homestead on the main road between Nicholville and Hopkinton.

The home, now owned by Jackie LesPerance, is a Victorian manor and was used as a bed & breakfast called "Chateau LesPerance" until recently. It was built in 1810 by Eliphalet Brush, one of Hopkinton's original settlers hailing from Vermont, and passed on to his son Jason who remodeled it in 1840. The elegant style he incorporated into the home is still apparent today. Jason married, ominously, another Olivia—Olivia Chittenden—in 1856. Two years and one child later she presumably died in her home—she presumably died in *that* home—at the young age of twenty-six. Genealogical records indicate that the couple had a child; however, no mention of the child's name can be found, nor any mention of what caused the premature death of Olivia Brush. We could speculate that she died during, or shortly after, childbirth, as was so common in those days.

Sketch from Evert's History of St. Lawrence County (1878) *depicting Brush homestead.*

The house eventually came to the ownership of family descendant Charles Brush, and it was during his tenure in the house that the infamous Goodnow murder occurred. The unfortunate victim's spirit is said to still dwell within the walls of the stately manor, determinedly bound to the earthly dimension until the mysterious circumstances surrounding her death are resolved, until her business here is finished, or until her wayward lover returns to take her away.

At the time of her death, Olivia was engaged to a Nicholville scoundrel named John Griffis and had told Mrs. Brush she would be leaving soon. However, Mr. Griffis had different plans. He had been telling people he wasn't quite ready to get married. On the eve of her untimely demise, Mr. Griffis had come to the Brush home to call on Olivia. After playing cards with the young couple, the others in the household retired, leaving Olivia and John alone in the living room. The next time the Brushes saw Olivia, she was dead on the couch, and Mr. Griffis was nowhere to be found. It was later learned that he had fled quickly that night and caught a train to New York City, never to be heard from again, except under the alias of H. L. Smith in two letters to his mother. In those letters, he said Olivia was dead before he left her at the house that night. The full content of the letters, however, has never been disclosed. Therefore, much of what happened that night is hypothetical, based on the following indisputable facts.

It seems Olivia had been in a 'delicate way.' According to a newspaper account dated March 25, 1901, in Potsdam's *Courier and Freeman*, "the girl had submitted to a delicate operation about a week or ten days before . . . at the hands of some skillful person." She had taken at least two drugs the night of her death, one possibly being corrosive in nature and the other presumably morphine obtained by John Griffis that night from a doctor in Nicholville to alleviate her suffering. The article stated that, "As the doctors progressed with the autopsy, they became more and more reticent as facts came to light showing the seriousness of the case, and at the close of the autopsy, all that could be obtained from them directly was that foul play was suspected and that the girl came to her death by criminal means and perhaps at the hands of her lover." The story continued that, "from the position of the body on the couch, it would seem highly improbable that she died after Griffis left, but was dead and partly laid out on the couch before he went away. The pillows were arranged smoothly and the deceased laid out on her back with no distortion of any part of the body. Mrs. Brush said the deceased was dressed in a red shirtwaist, black wool skirt, red underskirt, and cotton undergarments. When she first saw the body, she noticed the girl's corsets, shoes, apron and collar had been removed. The waist was unfastened and outer skirt pulled down firmly over the limbs and tucked under the right knee, in a way that could hardly have been done by the girl herself, and the underskirt was rolled up about the body under the upper skirt. Mrs. Brush also discovered stains upon the skirt which she was positive were not there during the evening previous."

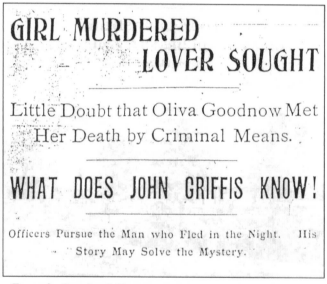

GIRL MURDERED
LOVER SOUGHT

Little Doubt that Oliva Goodnow Met Her Death by Criminal Means.

WHAT DOES JOHN GRIFFIS KNOW!

Officers Pursue the Man who Fled in the Night. His Story May Solve the Mystery.

From the Courier & Freeman *newspaper, March 25, 1901.*

"The condition of the girl's clothing, which it is impossible to fully describe, leads to the belief that abortion was attempted that night. What the autopsy revealed is known only to the doctors and officers. As near as can be ascertained, the theory of the prosecution is that the girl and her assistant had made preparations for that night and possibly had prepared themselves with drugs and other agencies for the consummation of the deed."

While it was not generally felt that John Griffis was guilty of deliberately murdering the woman who would be his bride, he was certainly guilty of leaving the scene of the crime and, thus, leaving the circumstances surrounding the crime a mystery to this day. He was last traced to Grand Central Station in New York City, where the trail was lost forever. The truth of what really happened that night went with John Griffis (a.k.a. H. L. Smith) to the grave.

Jackie LesPerance believes Olivia's benevolent spirit remains. She and her husband occasionally heard the sound of someone walking around in the house when they were in bed. The sound of footsteps upstairs was once so distinct, in fact, that the late Mr. LesPerance, a retired policeman, searched the house with his gun, looking for the intruder. Of course, none was seen.

Lights have been turned on and off by unseen hands. Mrs. LesPerance once found herself engaged in a playful exchange when she repeatedly attempted to turn off the dining room lights, only to find them quickly turned back on again. The mysterious banter continued until she finally convinced the guilty party to behave and let her rest.

Her copper bathtub sometimes shows the telltale discoloration that occurs soon after filling and emptying it, even right after she has cleaned and buffed it. It's as if someone has just taken a bath, when nobody has.

Her visiting daughter woke up one night to find her baby boy babbling to someone while the crib he was in seemed to rock by itself. Was it Olivia Goodnow, the unfortunate servant girl who found herself pregnant by the man she intended to marry? Or could it have been Olivia Brush, the ill-fated young mother, who died when her only child was but an infant a half a century before the Goodnow murder?

Whoever it is, visitors have felt her quiet presence when she opened their guest room doors, lingered for a moment, then left. Perhaps she was checking to see if the spineless Mr. Griffis had finally returned to claim his bride.

31

The House at the Racket

Racket River

If houses could hear, this house has surely heard the panicked cries of a man who drowned in the river behind the house. It would have heard the tortured sobs and ensuing silence of the many fatal car accidents nearby. It would have heard the primal wailing of native ancestors as they held down their fort in an unsettled land. It would certainly have heard the terrified shrieks of the young children upstairs as they fended off presences, both seen and unseen, even as those very presences tried to stifle their screams.

The small, unassuming house, more than sixty years old, is located in an early hamlet of Massena known, aptly, as Racket River. It sits at the spot of one of the Indian stockades erected along the Racquette a thousand or two years ago, when the St. Lawrence, Grasse, and Racquette Rivers were the highways of the natives. It was built by an ancestor of one of the earliest families to settle at Racket River and has been bought and sold many times since its construction, typically changing hands every couple of years. It may be that the family who spoke of it anonymously was not the only family to experience its particular brand of vengeance. It seems as if some homes have absorbed so much negative energy over the years that the walls and the floors are almost palpably pulsating with the dark secrets and heavy emotions that they hold. This is such a house.

Gracie was an energetic, towheaded toddler when her family moved into that house in 1964. One of her earliest memories is of waking one night in fear, feeling some uninvited presence in the room with her. She was about five years old at the time and sharing the upstairs bedroom with four-year-old Julie, and Lisa, who was six. She tried to scream, as her eyes adjusted to the light cast from the praying boy night-light, but the large, shadowy figure came out of the darkness at her and put a hand over her mouth and nose until she stopped trying to call out to her parents. The figure then vanished. The strange episode repeated itself several times over the next three years.

Julie was a slight, sensitive youngster when the night terrors began. For over a year, every night without fail, her terrified cries would rouse her exhausted mother and father from their slumber and bring them upstairs to her bedside. There they would find her in a baffling, inconsolable fit, fending off with her tiny hands that which only she could see, an evil and relentless intruder in her dreams. Tiny blisters formed around the cuticles of her little fingernails during each night terror, as if they were the manifesting proof of the heated battle she was waging in her sleep. All that her helpless parents could do was hold her tightly until the episode was over, wipe the tears away, and tuck her back in. She would awaken each morning, none the worse for wear, recalling not a bit of her nightly ordeals. Her fingertips were mysteriously healed until the next night terror, when it would start all over again. It's interesting to note that the night terrors that had occurred so regularly ceased abruptly the very day the family moved out of that home.

The upstairs consisted of just the one bedroom that the young sisters shared. At each end of the bedroom was a window. In the center of the bedroom, built into the attic wall, was a cubbyhole, blocked off by a loose sheet of plywood. None of the sisters recalls ever delving too deeply into it, for fear would stop them in their tracks every time they tried to peer past the plywood. Somehow, they felt certain that the perpetrator of their nightly ordeals resided within that space. Even now, more than thirty years later, Lisa, the oldest, has a fear of open closets, because it reminds her of the cubbyhole. Attached to the outside of the cubbyhole on one side was a storage unit with a sheet of plywood as its lid. Gracie decided that she wanted to move her mattress on top of that compartment, since it looked to be the size of a twin bed. It looked like it would be fun to sleep there. But one night, as she lay there with her cat, she heard a voice and thought, in her foggy near-sleep state, that it must be the cat somehow talking. The voice told her someone was going to pull her hair. Just then her head was jerked back violently by her hair. Lisa, too, felt the malicious hands on her head on more than one occasion as she lay helplessly in bed, paralyzed by fear.

Almost nightly, Lisa saw the graceful arm of a woman, cleanly dismembered just below the shoulder, hovering and moving gently in the light above her nightlight. She was not afraid of it, though; because, unlike the other menacing presences she felt or saw in that room, the arm was not at all threatening. It was just *there*. She became so used to seeing it, in fact, that she recalls being surprised one night to find that the hand was wearing a ring that she had not noticed before. In hindsight, she wonders now if the arm might have belonged to a young lady who was killed and mutilated in a tragic car accident next to their house, one of several fatal car accidents that occurred at that spot while the family lived there.

The parents might have believed the nightly antics going on upstairs were merely due to the apparently very active imaginations of their lot, but they also sensed something unsettling about the house. There was an eerie, continuous cold spot in the stairs leading to the upstairs bedroom where the girls slept. No matter how hot and humid the day, nor how well-heated the house was in the winter, that one spot part way up the stairs held a steady chill and was very disturbing to walk through. The decision was finally made to close off the upstairs, board it up, and have the three young girls share a small room on the first floor, just outside the bedroom of their parents.

Everyone seemed to sleep a little better, now that they were away from the attic and closer to the watchful eye of their parents. The house, or the invisible evil it appeared to contain within its walls, however, wasn't quite finished with them yet. One day, Gracie and Julie dutifully ran around the house, kissing every doorknob, and when their exasperated mother told them to stop and asked them why they were doing that, they matter-of-factly said it was because the Indian boy told them to. They had no way of knowing that the house sat on an ancient Indian stockade, so where would they have come up with such an excuse? Another day, when the girls were playing with the neighborhood children in the backyard, along a fence that prevented them from dropping off into the river, they all heard a loud, deep voice that seemed to come out of a sinkhole in the ground. It yelled at them to "Get out! Get out of here *now*!" At first, each child thought that one of them must have somehow said it, but then as they looked at each other in puzzlement, they heard it again, and they all ran up the hill screaming.

The family moved after six years of disturbing events, when they could finally take no more. Though the house continues to be sold repeatedly, it is hoped that the forces within that ruthlessly preyed upon innocent souls have somehow been completely vanquished in the years since this story took place.

The Haunting of Haskell House

Massena

Photo by author

Haskell House as it appears today.

Barry ran his fingertips slowly along the edge of the cradle he was making in the basement, checking to see if the wood was smooth enough where he had just fitted some pieces together. His friend Tommy worked alongside him, until he was summoned to take a phone call upstairs. As Tommy disappeared around the corner at the top of the stairs, the electric sander suddenly turned on. It was sitting on the far side of the basement in the dark, not being used. Barry was alone in the basement. He glanced up the steps to make sure his friend was indeed upstairs and did a double take to the far corner of the basement where the sander lay. Then he felt the blood drain from his face as the realization hit him, and he bolted up the stairs after his friend. The Captain, as he was known, was at it again. Apparently, he felt the cradle could use a little polishing.

"Captain" Lemuel Haskell built the historic house at 28 Tamarack Street in 1826 at the site of a sawmill along the Grasse River that he purchased from Amable Faucher and developed to prosperity. It is the oldest structure in Massena still being used as a dwelling, and it holds the distinction of being the site of Massena's first settlement, known in 1792 as the "Mile Square" and later as the "Haskell Square Mile." Captain Haskell and his wife Polly had three young children when they moved into the house: Laura, Martha, and Abel. Polly died in 1850, and the Captain died twenty years later, leaving the homestead to his son Abel, until his demise in 1909, when it was passed on to his descendants.

During World War I, the home was acquired by Alcoa and used to house workmen who were brought in to work at the plant. Then it was used as a house of worship by the Pilgrims Holiness Society, and after that as a multi-family dwelling. Barry Verville recalls that one of the tenants of the early sixties suffered a tragic loss when their teenage daughter was shot and killed by her mentally handicapped brother in the kitchen. In the early seventies, Joseph Verville, owner of Verville's Flower Shop, purchased the house, which by now had quite a colorful past. Mr. Verville set out to restore and modernize the structure while renting it out to several families. Ultimately, the old Haskell House came into the hands of its current owners, Barry and Allison Verville and their three children. This is their story.

Driving toward this stately old stone house, one can't help but imagine what life was like for its earliest residents. The solid, square structure stands as sturdy today as it did 174 years ago, tucked neatly into a curve between houses on Tamarack Street, off East Orvis Street in Massena. The outside walls are made of Grasse River limestone cut three feet thick. Heavy, local hand-hewn timbers of pine were used in construction throughout the dwelling. And, as if that weren't impressive enough, there is a legend of a half-million dollars being buried somewhere within the walls more than a hundred years ago by Lemuel Haskell himself, who made a small fortune running the mill. Though many have tried over the years to locate the money without demolishing the property, none have succeeded. Barry and Allison, while enjoying the mystery of the tale, have no plans to tear up their sound historical home searching for the elusive buried cash that may—or may not—be there. Although, Allison won't deny her anticipation at finding a loose block in the outside wall, and reaching inside to see if she had stumbled upon the lost treasure or a map showing its whereabouts! She found neither.

Nobody knows for certain that the Captain is the one haunting their home—it actually could be any of a number of possibilities including the Captain or Mrs. Haskell, Abel Haskell, or the young girl who died in the kitchen. However, the Verville's prefer to fondly blame the occasional mischief on the architect, builder, and first resident of the legendary house—none other than Captain Haskell himself. Family and friends alike have experienced temperature extremes in the house, walking through areas that are uncharacteristically chilly—a common phenomenon of ghostly encounters—or hot. When it was discovered that the thermostat on the first floor was being deliberately manipulated, the Verville family at first blamed one another until they finally accepted the fact that it was not one of them, but rather an unseen hand. Now, they casually say, "The Captain did it," whenever something unexplained like that happens. This could work to their children's advantage, more so than for children living in your average un-haunted house. After all, how many times have we, as parents, said, "It must've been a ghost, then!" when our children fervently deny any wrongdoing? In the case of Haskell House, it's perfectly possible that a ghost actually did do it.

Modern plumbing also seems to hold some appeal for the Captain, and why shouldn't it? After all, indoor toilets had not yet been invented when the Haskell House was built, and even at the time of his death in 1870, Americans were still scurrying to create a satisfactory indoor flushable commode. Indoor plumbing, bathtubs, and separate washrooms had yet to make their debut. The Haskell's likely used an outhouse and bathed weekly by the woodstove in the kitchen, like others of their day. Peach, the Verville's pretty daughter, has heard the toilet upstairs in the next room flush when nobody is in there, presumably of the Captain's doing. On another occasion, when Barry and Allison and their sister and brother-in-law tried to put in a new kitchen faucet, the meddling Captain caused the seemingly impossible to happen. The faucet handles were in the off position, yet the water ran. The water even ran when the water main was turned off! When the main water supply was turned back on, the water refused to run, and so on. The four witnesses shook their heads in disbelief at the bizarre scene on display before them. Playing with fixtures is a fairly common ghostly antic, it seems. Not only does it get the attention of the living, but the novelty of these amazing modern toys of ours must also make them particularly attractive to old-time ghosts—like offering a lighter to a caveman.

In keeping with the tradition of stereotypical ghostly behavior, objects get inexplicably moved or *re*moved in Haskell House. For example, a television set in the living room positioned in front of one of the original five fireplaces that have long since been sealed off had a hexagon clock that sat on top of it. Each morning Barry would find the clock facing toward the left and would straighten it, only to find it again repositioned the next day. The odd exchange finally ceased when he moved the television set away from the fireplace and to another part of the living room. Perhaps Captain Haskell's favorite chair had been to the left of the fireplace, and he couldn't see the time from that angle. But that doesn't say much for the theory that time is irrelevant in the spirit world.

The Captain—stubbornly adhering to his long ago 'man of the house' title—also once seemed a bit put off at having bags of groceries set on the sturdy coffee table in the living room. Maybe it hadn't left enough room for him to prop his spectral legs up on the table to warm his bones before a phantom fire, no doubt while sitting in his favorite chair of yesteryear and looking at the clock that he kept positioning just so! One day Allison placed several bags of groceries down on the coffee table in the living room and went into the kitchen to make some coffee for herself and a friend named Trudi, when she heard Mata, their beloved German shephard dog, barking anxiously. Back in the living room, Mata rushed gratefully to her side and a heavy bag of groceries was found lying on the floor. The bag had been in the middle of the table, amid other bags. It would've been impossible from its internal position for it to tip off the table without disturbing the other bags. Mata would not leave Allison's side after that little commotion. She even refused to follow her upstairs and was right underfoot whenever Allison took her into the basement to do laundry. The ghost seemed to wander the whole house, and Mata sensed it acutely.

While the Verville family has become used to their resident ghost, friends and relatives are sometimes a little uneasy with the feelings they get of being watched or followed in the house. Allison's sister, for example, refuses to sleep in the bedroom upstairs when she visits, opting instead to sleep in the cozy living room downstairs. Of course, the living room is as haunted as any other room in the house.

For everyone who is drawn to the mystery of a haunted house, an equal number of people will avoid one at all costs for the same reason. Often there is nothing tangible to validate one's fear of being haunted, just a 'feeling' that they are not alone; however, there was one situation in the attic at Haskell House that would justify even a skeptic's apprehension.

Barry's brother-in-law was doing construction in the attic and had nailed a sheet of plywood across the opening to prevent curious children from roaming in where dangerous tools lay strewn about so he could go downstairs for a minute. Incredibly, when he returned a few minutes later, the nails had all been pried loose and the board blocking the attic removed and set aside. There had been nobody else up there while he was downstairs. It was added to the list of mysterious happenings at Haskell House.

Though Haskell House is widely known for its historical significance and its legend of buried treasure, here's something that wasn't as well-known until now: The Captain is a ghost!

Too Hot to Handle

Baxterville

Photo by Diane Murphy
Murphy home before the fire.

It was a night Diane and Fred Murphy will never forget. They had gone out for the evening, as they usually did each weekend, but on that night they decided to try someplace different. For that reason, nobody knew where to find them when their house caught on fire around six o'clock. It was a horrible shock to return to what was left of their home nearly eight hours later, and even more of a shock when a weary fireman approached them to say he was very sorry, but they were not able to save the Murphys' grandmother in the fire.

Diane and Fred looked at each other. *What grandmother?* No grandmother lived with them, and nobody had been in their home while they were away. Still, the fireman insisted that there was an old woman they clearly saw screaming in the upstairs window. It was a night the local firefighters would also never forget.

About three months earlier, Diane had gone to the Norfolk Museum to research the history of the red brick farmhouse they lived in on West Hatfield Street in a hamlet of Norfolk known as the Baxterville area, just outside of Massena. Besides finding out that the earliest occupants of her home had been notorious for their gambling, brawling, and womanizing ways, she was also told of a trap door in the cellar that led to a room on the first floor—a room you could access only through the cellar. It was suggested to her that during Prohibition, people may have carried bootlegged whisky up from the Racquette River, which is across the road, and sold it in the hidden room, where they could quickly conceal their covert activities if the need arose. Diane wanted to know if that room and the trap door still existed.

In their nine years in the home, Fred and Diane had never noticed a trap door in the cellar. They did notice the old timber joists on the ceiling of the basement, but the trap door was now hidden behind wires and pipes and was inaccessible to them. Diane's curiosity couldn't be contained any longer, and when Fred was away for a few days, she used a hammer to tear the wall down. Sure enough, behind it was a closet-size room, akin to a roadside lemonade stand. She could easily visualize a little clandestine operation in there, even though the room was now stripped of its previously prohibited contents.

In her haste to satisfy her curiosity, however, she hadn't thought about the possible consequences of her actions. Besides Fred's understandable lack of enthusiasm at finding a wall missing when he got home, it seems someone else wasn't very thrilled about the impromptu remodeling of their home either. Diane recalls that after she tore down "that wall" was when "all hell broke loose."

There was the time when she went home for lunch and, quickly tidying up, picked up a coffee mug that someone had left out on the counter to put in the dishwasher. But the cup was too hot to hold, which was very odd, because nobody had been home for hours before she got there. She tried to pick the cup up again a half hour later as she was getting ready to go back to work, but it still remained too hot to handle. It finally had cooled off by the time she returned home that evening.

Another unexplained incident happened one night when her daughter and a friend, both teenagers at the time, came home and announced that they wanted pizza. Since nobody delivered pizza that far out of town at that time, Diane told them they'd have to settle for sandwiches. Later that night, Diane woke up around three A.M. and went into the kitchen. There, on the table, was a pizza box with two pieces of pizza and a knife inside. She would take the matter up with her daughter in the morning, she figured. So the next morning, Diane went to her daughter's room, where the two plates with breadcrumbs from sandwiches were in plain sight, and she asked her daughter where the pizza box was. There was no sign of the box or the knife anywhere in the house, and she wanted to know how her daughter managed to get it, when she wasn't old enough to drive. Mildly annoyed, her daughter quickly reminded her that she wouldn't let them get pizza, so they only had the sandwiches Diane had made for them.

Another time, like something out of "The Twilight Zone," their answering machine was the object of possible paranormal tampering. Diane came home and pressed the button that indicates the number of messages waiting. It typically flashes once for every message received, but that day it was flashing repeatedly, as if the machine's limit for messages had been reached. Like many answering machines, theirs allowed a minute for each message before it was automatically cut off. Strangely, when Diane pressed the button to play back her messages, however, she got an earful of just one long message that ran the entire length of the tape.

She heard a disturbing confrontation between a woman and a man, with the woman saying, "It's all your fault I'm pregnant," and the man telling her to shut her mouth, followed by a loud slap, and the woman saying, "I can't take it anymore." Diane said it was as if someone from within the room itself were using just the tape-recording function of the answering machine. Nothing else can explain the isolated incident with the machine, and it has never acted that way again. The unsolved mysteries were beginning to mount, but the climax was yet to come.

On the night of the fire back in 1991, local volunteer firefighters were horrified to see an old woman in the upstairs window—in the very bedroom where the fire originated. The woman, screaming and banging frantically on the windowpane, had gray hair that was pulled up in a bun, and she was wearing a dress with polka dots on it. It was a fireman's worst nightmare, and it was their first priority to get to that bedroom first. When they finally reached it, however, there was no sign of the woman—only piles of ashes, as you would expect in such a devastating fire. Their heroic efforts had been in vain, and the firefighters realized they had to impart a double dose of bad news to Fred and Diane when they returned home.

Dread turned to relief when Fred and Diane told the firefighters that nobody else lived with them and the house had been unoccupied while they were away. Relief quickly turned to bewilderment when the firefighters realized that whomever they had seen in the upstairs window had not been a living person, and the only explanation was that she was a ghost. It was the talk of the town for a while, and Diane was later told by another person who had been on the scene that night that "everyone had seen" the lady in the window, and they had been frantic to get to her.

Several weeks later, a fire was set to level what remained of the structure so that the Murphys could rebuild on the property. They took photographs of the controlled burn so they would remember the moment that spelled both closure and a new beginning in their lives.

To their amazement, one of the photographs revealed the woman in the window. It was in the downstairs living room window this time, though, and the woman was sadly looking downward. The photograph was passed from hand to hand and somewhere along the line, it got misplaced and has never been found. But seeing it, and hearing the related story of the woman in the window, was enough to convince many non-believers in the afterlife.

The Murphys new home is attractive and modern and sits slightly behind the spot where their former home had been at 75 West Hatfield Street. The basement of the old home was filled in with topsoil after the controlled burn, and there is now no sign of the original house ever having been there.

Grandma and Her Dog

Louisville

"Jack, come back!" they yelled, but he was racing excitedly toward the other side—the other side of the road, that is.

The driver couldn't possibly have stopped in time. You know how fast those little dogs can run when they're on a mission. Standing at just over a foot tall, it's a wonder you could see the tiny fur balls at all if they ran out in front of you. And this boy was cruising, intent on reaching his destination, wherever that was. It was as if he spotted someone he loved, but witnesses said they could see nobody on the other side of the road. They watched, helpless, as the unstoppable pup made haste, his long crème-colored fur a blur as it flowed in the breeze his speed created. It was the day his beloved master was to be buried. Now there would be two burials.

Brenda's grandmother-in-law, Winnie, lived in a housing complex for the elderly in a small community just south of Massena. Jack had been her pampered Lhasa apso and her sole companion at the time of her death. Brenda thinks that perhaps the old woman had called to Jack on the day he ran out in front of a car so they could be together eternally.

On the day Winnie died, Brenda and her three-year-old daughter had paid her a visit, as they often did. Brenda was very fond of her husband's grandmother, having hit if off from the day they met. Winnie asked Brenda to come back that evening and spend the night with her, after her husband got home at ten to stay with their daughter. Although the request was unusual, Brenda agreed. Then a short time later, Winnie called her back and told her not to worry about going

49

over that night, after all. Instead, pick an evening when she could go earlier and have more time to visit. That was the last time anyone spoke to her. She passed away that night. Brenda believes Winnie knew she was about to die, because she had been giving away little trinkets for three days.

Winnie's body was placed in the vault until spring, when the ground thawed and she could be properly buried. The day after her funeral, Brenda and her friend, Karen, went up to Winnie's apartment to clean and get it in order before her daughters came by to empty it out. It was stuffy in the small one-bedroom apartment, because Winnie "smoked like a chimney" for years, so after a while, Brenda propped the door to the balcony open with an upright vacuum and went back to work with Karen. While they were cleaning the kitchen, they heard the front door click shut, so Brenda went out to prop it back open again, figuring a breeze must've moved the vacuum enough for the door to close. When she opened the door, the vacuum was gone, the air was still, and there was nobody around. Brenda and Karen were baffled. Eventually, they found the vacuum in the bathroom, which was six feet away and around a corner, and the bathroom door had closed behind it. The girls knew the bathroom door had been open, because they were airing it out after Karen mopped the floor in there. Karen promptly informed Brenda that she was ready to leave right then, if not sooner.

Two weeks later, Grandma made her presence known again, only this time it was at Brenda's own house. The two women, Brenda and Winnie, shared the same birth date, and it was on the evening of her birthday that Brenda was awakened by what she thought was her daughter calling her for a drink. As she sat up, she saw Winnie hovering mid-air behind the little TV that sat diagonally on a stand in the corner of their bedroom. Unable to speak, Brenda elbowed her husband, and he sat up asking what was wrong. Then he briefly saw it, too. He rubbed his eyes and looked again, just as they do on TV when they can't believe what they're seeing. The form was still there, but only for a second. In a blink, she was gone. Was Winnie visiting to her favorite granddaughter-in-law to wish her a happy birthday?

Several weeks later, the weekend before the official burial, Winnie's daughter Fran was taking a break from spring cleaning to sit down and write the obituary that would go in the newspaper in Oswego where Winnie was to be buried. Deep in thought about her deceased mother, she jumped when the bottle of Windex on the desk in front of her suddenly sprayed the window all by itself right before her eyes. Needless to say, Fran was flabbergasted.

Besides her obvious glee at pulling pranks on hapless housekeepers as they work, Winnie seems to be constantly on the go, getting around well for an old woman—even if she is a ghost. Her presence has been felt in her own apartment, at her daughter's home, and at her granddaughter-in-law's home. And she may well have been by the side of the road, as well—on the day Jack went to meet his maker, and his master.

The House on Liberty Avenue

Massena

"Hi, Meghan? This is Cheri. You left a message for me to call?"

"Yes, hi. I wanted to give you an update on our situation. Some people came over last night who are able to communicate with spirits, and they told me there's a ghost trapped in the stairwell!"

And that was not the half of it.

In 1907, Alcoa created Liberty Avenue and the surrounding streets in the village of Massena on which to build modern housing to sell to employees who were being shipped in for plant construction. Since then, of course, most of the homes have been fitted with new siding and completely renovated, leaving only the foundations and basic structures in their original states. The homes on the north end of the street are spaced perhaps fifteen feet apart and share a similar form—mostly two-story, vinyl-sided homes. Meghan and Matt Sharlow's home is unremarkable in its outward appearance—neat and modest like the houses on either side—but what is going on behind closed doors sets it apart from all the others.

Their eighteen-month-old son, Mikey, was the first to sense it. Soon after the Sharlow's moved their young family into the house on Liberty Avenue, they noticed that Mikey was behaving strangely. He would look down the stairwell and scream as if something was scaring him, and most nights for the few weeks while it lasted, he was inconsolable and refused to go to bed until the wee hours of the morning. One time during one of these nightly crying fits, Matt saw what appeared to be a dark shadow flowing up the stairs, almost as if it was a part of the stairs itself, barely perceptible to the human eye. There was no form, just a slithery shadow gliding along the steps. He wondered if his eyes were playing tricks on him. He would know soon enough.

While the nightly episodes of crying have thankfully subsided, Mikey has begun exhibiting new signs of unusual behavior. He acts like he has an imaginary playmate; at least, that's what an observer's first inclination would be. He talks casually to someone he calls Joshua. Someone his parents can't see. Whenever you ask him where Joshua is, he looks around for him. He takes Joshua's hand and is guided through the house. When he holds Joshua's hand, he doesn't stumble or put his little arms out for balance like he would if he was toddling about alone. He maneuvers through doorways without so much as touching the doorframe. All the while, his arm is raised and extended as he holds onto Joshua's invisible hand and looks up into Joshua's invisible eyes. And he obediently does whatever Joshua tells him to do.

One time when he was eating noodles in his high chair, he looked over toward the gate at the entrance to the living room and said, "What? Okay." He put some noodles on his fork and held the fork out. Then, with a confused look on his face, he set the food off to the side of the tray in a neat little pile. It was as if Joshua was saying, "Hey, Mikey, save some of that for me, would you? No, no...I can't come and get it right now, just set it aside and save it, okay?" Another time, Mikey looked over at the gate where Joshua seems to hang out and said, "Okay." Then he toddled over to the gate and opened it effortlessly, something he supposedly didn't know how to do yet. Matt believes he sees Joshua, too, as a dark, evasive shadow that seems to peek around the corner of the living room sometimes at night, but ducks away when Matt approaches it. Could it be the same invisible prankster who turns light switches on and off right before Matt's eyes? Or who moves shoes around, always in pairs, neatly arranging them in the most unlikely places? Certainly a baby can't be blamed for such mischief, and Matt and Meghan know they aren't the ones doing it.

The plot thickened one day when Meghan confided in a neighbor about the strange goings-on in their apartment. With their houses being of identical design and the upstairs windows perfectly aligned, the neighbor was able to see easily into the Sharlow's home. That is how, the perceptive neighbor explained, she once noticed a young girl walk out of Matt and Meghan's bedroom and down the hall, stopping once to look back at her. A little boy then ran after the girl, and, like that, they were gone. She thought it was peculiar because she knew those children didn't live there. Neither does the woman Matt briefly mistook for his wife one day. He did a double take when he noticed the strangely attired woman glide toward the dresser in their bedroom with her back to him. It wasn't until he called to her, and she vanished before his eyes, that he realized it wasn't Meghan. Well, that, and the fact that his wife didn't wear her hair in an elegant high bun or glide across rooms very often!

At the end of her rope, Meghan was eager to get to the bottom of what she calls the "freaky" incidents, so she and her husband gratefully accepted the help of a local psychic who is able to sense and communicate with spirit. He is also a gifted healer and performs spirit rescue and exorcisms. With little prior knowledge of their situation, the man was able to walk into the house on Liberty and quickly confirm some of what the Sharlow's already suspected but hadn't mentioned. He saw Mikey's friend, Joshua. He explained that Joshua is like a guardian to their son, and he will go with the family if they move and will stay with their son until he is no longer needed. The imaginary friend, it turns out, is a concerned and protective spirit and is not so imaginary after all. He told Matt and Meghan that Mikey is a very gifted and sensitive child himself. That is why he is able to see spirits when those around him can't. There are also two young spirits in the residence, confirming what the neighbor had seen through the upstairs window. The two children and their mother died in a tragic fire in that home many years before. The mother is an older spirit who mostly dwells in the master bedroom. She is who Matt saw when he first thought it was his wife. The description the psychic gave matched Matt's description of the woman exactly. The deceased woman takes it upon herself to watch over Matt and Meghan's infant daughter, just as Joshua watches over Mikey.

Finally, the healer found an ornery old guy 'trapped' in the stairwell, by his own volition. This spirit fervidly refuses to budge and has claimed the stairs as his space. Although he never lived in the house, he did visit and fall down the stairs there, possibly causing an injury that ultimately led to his demise. He refuses to allow the spirit of the older woman in the master bedroom to go down 'his' stairs, causing much agitation between the two, because it confines the female spirit to the upstairs of what she feels is still her own home. She may have been the woman of the house when the fall occurred, and he seeks his spiteful revenge by playing out this eternal rivalry between the two. He intends no harm, however, toward the current residents; his gripe is purely with the female spirit. Mikey is able to see the spirit of the man, and he knows that the old codger doesn't want anyone going near the stairs. It would be enough to keep a brave adult awake at night, let alone a toddler!

Having their suspicions confirmed explains many things, like why Mikey behaves so strangely, why a dark shadow is sometimes seen slithering up the stairway or peeking around corners, and why people from another place and time have been seen in their house. But if you just found out you had five ghosts living in your house, including one sourpuss you had to walk through every time you wanted to go up or down the stairs—even though it shed some light on your situation—would you sleep better or worse?

If the dead can't rest in peace, how on earth can the living?

Worse Things Could Happen

Knapps Station

There's a big old house on Dry Bridge Road in the little hamlet of Knapps Station, between Norfolk and Stockholm. If you drive by, you might see the front door occasionally ajar, even when it appears that nobody is around. Don't blame it on the tenants; they never forget to lock the door, but they often find it open when they return home from their outings. Maybe someone, or something, has left the house to seek out others when its usual victims are not around to prey on. Or maybe it's just keeping the door half open in anticipation of their return.

Rachel and Carly have never forgotten what went on in that house when Carly lived there a few years ago. There were unexplained voices and footsteps, smells, and images, and explosive encounters. It actually got so bad for various tenants over the years that the owners brought in priests, psychics, and even an Indian shaman; but nothing has helped so far. It's just an "evil house" according to Rachel, and she still get chills whenever she thinks about it.

One night the two women were walking through the dining room to the living room. They suddenly heard a very loud and clear woman's voice yell, "Carly!" They just looked at each other, realizing that it wasn't a familiar voice but still hoping desperately that it was Carly's roommate, Breanna. They yelled up to Brea, as they called her, and she told them that it wasn't her; she had been almost asleep, listening to soft music in her room. It wouldn't be the last time the women heard unexplained voices or their names being called. In fact, it happened all the time; but there were worse things

57

that could happen to them—and they did.

Carly and Brea often sat on the couch in the living room chatting. The house was very quiet, on one such occasion, with no music playing and the television turned off. Mid-sentence, Carly happened to glance at the TV, which was directly across from them, and what she saw made her blood run cold. There was a man sitting between the two of them smiling wickedly. Carly found enough of her voice to whisper to Brea not to say a word, but to just look into the TV between the two of them. Brea saw what Carly saw. Without another word, the two women looked at each other, got up and ran from the house, unsure of what to make of the frightening incident.

On a whim, Rachel and a friend went down into the basement one day, just to see what it looked like—and maybe to test their courage a little, too. They got more than they bargained for. As they approached the landing at the bottom of the stairs, a foul smell started wafting toward them. It made Rachel sick to her stomach, but she was determined to continue on. With their hands covering their noses, they fumbled their way through the shadows to a wall, behind which an apparent room seemed to have been completely sealed off with blocks. Some of the blocks were broken or missing, as luck would have it, so they shone their flashlight into the holes to see if they could determine what exactly was behind the wall. The light from their flashlight was of no use, however. All they could see was pitch black, as if the light beam was swallowed up by the darkness. Rachel thinks that perhaps the room was a part of the Underground Railroad.

A friend who was staying at the house was asleep on a couch in the large second-floor corridor one evening when the sound of someone walking up the nearby stairway woke him. He turned to see who was there but saw nobody. Certain of what he had heard, he panicked and proceeded to wake everyone in the house to tell them of his ordeal. Misery loves company.

One day Rachel and Carly were in the bathroom getting ready to go out. They were casually discussing how evil the house was when the bathroom window began to rattle loudly. The women tore from the room, and right smack on their heels, the bathroom door was slammed shut by an unseen hand. The ferocity of it shook the entire house. It would be one of their most chilling encounters.

Rachel recalls that the house was always very cold, and there was a spot in the kitchen where you could stand and actually feel someone put a hand on your back. The house itself seemed to take hold of people as soon as they entered, according to Carly. The sense of evil was so strong that it pervaded their senses in every way and somehow pitted them against each other, causing tenants and visitors alike to fight each other for no reason, and then just as quickly make up. It was as if the house, or the spirit acting as puppet master, was amused at its power over those who entered, using them as mere pawns in some sort of nightmarish game.

So if you pass by a house on Dry Bridge Road and the door just happens to be open, don't you dare go near. It might be trying to draw you in to *play*.

Nightmare on Main Street

Potsdam

A Plattsburgh woman has a horrible dream of a fire that destroys a sorority house in Potsdam where her coworker's daughter, Tasha, currently lives. The fire is blamed on Tasha, a local college student, who moved into the house on Main Street in August of 2000. The woman keeps the dream to herself for several weeks, not wanting to worry those involved with the disturbing details.

During the same time period, unbeknownst to the dreamer, Tasha really was being besieged by mysterious, fire-related events in the house that she shared with four other girls. A burner on the gas stove was sometimes found fully lit in the middle of the night, but not by the hands of any of the young tenants. The modern stove had an electronic ignition system, and several steps were necessary to light a burner. Tasha, whose bedroom is closest to the kitchen, once heard the revealing double-click of a burner being turned on just before she noticed the kitchen aglow from the flame on the burner. Nobody was in the kitchen at the time. In another nearby bedroom, the smoke detector went off repeatedly at inappropriate times, even after being examined by the landlord. Incidentally, the landlord said there must have been a fire in the house at one time, because the attic beams were all charred.

If the ghostly pyromaniac in the kitchen didn't scare the living daylights out of the girls with its fire-starting antics, it certainly got their attention on another occasion when they all heard loud clattering noises coming from the kitchen. None of the frightened girls dared to move to investigate, opting instead to wait until daybreak, at which time they found dishes scattered about the floor.

Emma, whose bedroom is adjacent to Tasha's, was awakened once in the middle of the night when someone sat at the end of her bed. Puzzled, she quickly turned on the light, only to find that while no*body* was there, a distinct impression remained on her bed where someone had presumably sat. Mary—who also has a first-floor bedroom—and Tasha, once heard and saw the shadow of someone coming down from upstairs, but when they went out to see who it was, they found nobody there. Neither of the girls who sleep upstairs had stirred. Seeing shadows out of the corners of their eyes and the sense that they were being watched were experiences each girl could relate to.

They have all heard loud sounds that seemed to come from the walk-in closet in Tasha's room, when Tasha was not in there. The girls liken the sound to someone pounding on the ceiling of the closet with a broomstick. Inside of the closet is an old door that doesn't open and seems to lead nowhere. The girls decided to investigate. Tasha and her boyfriend pried open the door in her closet and found that the opening directly behind it had also been boarded up. Behind the house, they found a door that had been blocked with several other old doors nailed onto it. Had somebody tried to keep someone out . . . or someone *in* the house? Over the door was a window they managed to climb up to so they could peek in. What they saw was a barren, boarded up room with white and brown walls that appeared to have been a bathroom, minus the usual fixtures. It was another dead end, both structurally and figuratively. Climbing up to peer in through the window of a mysterious empty room that had been securely and haphazardly boarded up brought more questions than answers. It seemed the more they tried to pull together the pieces of this particular puzzle, the less they knew.

More curious than ever, they decided to go straight to the landlord. His wife told them that a three- or four-year-old girl had died in the house many years ago, but she didn't know how. Other sorority sisters who resided there some twenty years ago had reported ghostly activity to the landlord at that time. They claimed to have felt little hands touching them as if trying to get their attention. It was they who first researched the house and found out about the little girl who had died there. They learned that, as was commonplace in the olden days, her memorial service was held in the house. The question of how she died remains to be answered, but the following experiences may hold some chilling clues.

One night, while Mary and Tasha were quietly conversing in Tasha's room, they heard the cries of what sounded like a little girl coming from Emma's adjacent bedroom. They rushed in to find Emma, apparently talking in her sleep, curled up in a fetal position at the head of the bed in hysterics. In a small child's voice, she was crying for help, saying things like, "No. Help me. Go away. Get off me!" Astonished, they promptly shook their friend out of her delirious state. Once back to herself, Emma had no memory of the incident. Mary's boyfriend then experienced a similar situation in the house one night, and when Mary woke him, he was terrified. He told her he had been paralyzed by something evil that had been on top of him, crushing the very life out of him. Was the little girl who died in the house letting others experience her horrible demise so her death could be understood? Was she the victim of a cold-blooded killer?

Many questions remain with this house that is so clearly haunted. Why did the Plattsburgh woman have a dream about Tasha and a fire at the sorority house without even knowing of the events that were actually unfolding? Why did the stove keep igniting and the smoke alarm keep going off? Is it related in an ethereal sense to the fire that charred the attic beams? Why is the room behind the closet so tightly boarded up, and why is there pounding on the ceiling of the room? Why have people felt a little girl's hands on them and experienced her terror? Did human hands strangle her or did she die in a fire, clutching her own throat as the oxygen-deficient atmosphere slowly consumed her last breath? Why did she remain quiet for nearly twenty years and then choose that particular set of tenants to haunt?

Why, indeed?

It's Back . . . A Haunted Trailer

Lisbon

Mary knew she was getting a full package the day she married Michael in 1996. The moment the counselor said, "I do," she got a new husband, new stepchildren, a new home with new dogs in a new neighborhood. She had expected all of that and was pleased with the many changes occurring in her life. What she hadn't expected was a new ghost who was waiting in the wings.

Her new home was actually an old seventies-style mobile home—white with blue trim—which her husband had shared with his ex-wife and their children, but it was new to Mary. It was nestled in the dense woods on a remote dead-end road in Lisbon. Neighbors were few and far between, making it private and peaceful, and she loved it. So, what could explain the vague discomfort Mary felt in that home from the start? It wasn't that she was alone in the middle of nowhere. She had already mentally ruled that out. More likely it was because she was not the first woman her husband had shared the house, or his life, with. That must've been it. That was the root of her anxiety, she assured herself.

Her certainty dwindled shortly thereafter, however, when she heard a shrill scream in the hallway where she was vacuuming one day. Her husband, a police officer, consoled her as best he could with the suggestion that the shriek had probably come from a coy dog, not the insane maniac that it sounded like. After all, anyone who lives in the backwoods of these parts knows how chilling the sound of a coy dog, owl, or even a fox on the hunt is. Gratefully, Mary accepted his explanation and settled into her new surroundings without further concern, until 1997. Then things got really strange.

Mary began seeing shadows moving through the trailer, especially in the hallway near the bedrooms. She wondered if her imagination was working overtime. Then the trailer became difficult to heat. In fact, it was sometimes so cold, even on full heat, that she could see her breath. Maybe it was just too old to heat sufficiently, she had reasoned. But then the shadows became more noticeable. Finally, Mary had to concede that something was really going on, something that wasn't so easy to explain away.

When Mary told Michael what she was seeing and feeling, his face went pale. He shook his head and said, "It's back." He explained how he and his ex-wife had experienced many strange things in the house. At least three times, he heard his name called by a soft female voice—once when he was in the barn, once in the shower, and once outside in the yard. Each time he was alone, yet he heard his name clearly spoken. His son would sometimes scream in the night and tearfully point to a corner of his room, saying, "boo, boo." His daughter did the same when she had been in that room, which was used as a nursery for both children.

Michael and Mary agreed to wait and see if the ghost felt like a threat to them before they made any hasty decisions about moving out.

A few nights later, they were doing dishes when their son got up off the living room floor and walked trance-like toward their bedroom, saying "Dad" over and over again. Mary called to him and told him his father was in the kitchen right beside her, but the boy fervently assured them that he had watched his father walk into their bedroom. After that incident, they called a priest to come in and bless their house.

All was well until one night in October of 1999 when Mary was home alone, cleaning the kitchen. Her two normally complacent Labrador retrievers woke out of a sound sleep and began growling toward the hallway leading to the bedrooms. When Mary looked down the hallway to see what was causing the commotion, she witnessed the strangest thing she had ever seen. The floor-length tassels that hung from the doorway of her stepdaughter's bedroom were bent at a right angle midair, then stretched taut to the other side of the hallway. At the same time, Mary was overcome by a floral scent so strong that it caused heartburn. She immediately phoned Michael who told her to go to where he worked, but she didn't have enough gas in her vehicle to get that far. With her dogs by her side, she camped out under the kitchen table for nearly two hours until the scent faded completely away.

Again the house was blessed, and all was quiet in the house until November of 2000. Michael was away at military training, and Mary was in bed when she heard eerie and indescribable noises coming from her stepdaughter's room. Thankfully, they lasted only a few seconds, but it was long enough to let her know that 'it' was back once again. A few days later, when Michael was making toast, Mary saw him glance up at her curiously. A second later, as she reached to turn on a light in the living room, a bright flash went by her. The couple stood there stunned. Michael had heard the familiar soft woman's voice call his name just before they both saw the white streak. Who does that mysterious voice belong to? Perhaps she is the grandmother who died in the home years before Michael bought it. He was told that she cared for her grandchildren many nights there. That may explain one of the ghosts haunting the trailer. However, there appears to be others, like the male spirit who looked like Michael entering the master bedroom. His story is still a mystery, and maybe it always will be.

Recently Mary and Michael purchased a new mobile home, and their haunted trailer was removed from the property. They have yet to determine if their ghost was bound to the land or to the home itself. Time will tell.

Spanky's Diner

Massena

Spanky's Diner as it appears today.

Eddy tried to steady his trembling fingers to lock the diner door. It was no use, and he wasn't going to waste another precious second trying to secure the place. He turned and raced home, waiting until he was safe and sound in his own apartment before he called his boss. It was Eddy's first day of employment as a dishwasher on the night shift, and he had been alone for only a short time when he called it quits, literally. He told his boss, Valerie, that he would not be returning to work at the diner—ever—not after what he had heard that night. She wasn't entirely surprised. Working the night shift alone at the diner is a test of courage—a psychological "Toughman Competition," if you will. You see, the diner is quite haunted, and the turnover rate for the nighttime dishwashers is quite high.

Located at 3 North Main Street at the corner of Main and Center, Spanky's Diner is one of Massena's most charming and enduring diners. Known formerly as The Massena Diner and then simply as The Diner, it was purchased by Alex "Spanky" Krywanczyk over fifteen years ago and is managed by his daughter, Valerie LeValley. Massena's first hospital, owned and operated by Dr. Louis J. Calli, sat where Route 37B now lies, directly behind the diner and within very close proximity to the building. Across the street from the front of the diner are the choppy waters of the Grasse River and a bridge leading to the heart of downtown Massena.

The oldest part of the existing building was once an old railroad car that the late Al Nicola delivered to its current location to open as a small diner in 1956. This portion of the diner still houses the original retro bar stools that its earliest patrons sat on, and you are at once embraced by a strong air of nostalgia upon entering the room. You almost feel as if you can reach out and touch the past. But in actuality, the past is reaching out and touching you.

Ten years ago, after a story about the haunted diner was published in *The Pennysaver*, two local psychics were asked to investigate. They saw a slim, dark-haired girl in white who they felt had drowned in the river. Her name began with L. She appeared to be a happy-natured soul. There was a spirit of a man who was concerned with how well the diner was doing and kept a constant eye on everything. He could often be heard walking about the diner. Another spirit was a limping man whose leg and hip were somehow injured. Maybe he had been a patient at the old Calli hospital that had been practically in the diner's backyard. There was also a tall, older man with white hair who appeared to be a good soul.

As the psychics sat in the original section for lunch, they noticed a decided chill and could feel the spirits clustering around them. One spirit who was very prominent in the diner haunting at that time came forward and spoke to them. He said, "We need to communicate to tell all of you that we mean only to assist you. This is our restaurant, too. This lady tells us we are dead. We do not feel dead." He appeared to be a big, beefy, man with a black mustache who was generous and good-natured. He died of heart failure and looked to be in his late sixties. The name of Pat resounded as the psychic wrote her notes.

The spirits, according to the two psychics, were together to help each other. They were especially busy at night, as any evening shift employee, or even Alex himself, can attest to. Most of them hang around in the basement, where one of the psychics saw a flash of white and a partial figure that disappeared in front of the washing machine. Other spirits mentioned during the investigation were Yvonne, Wesley, and William. One of them bluntly announced, "We do not haunt. We inhabit."

Recently, Alex allowed another group of eight psychic individuals to investigate his haunted diner. They included Ronnie Guindon of Toronto; Marjorie Thorpe of Cornwall, Ontario; and Joanne Deruchia of Massena. Armed with varying abilities, a 35mm Minolta camera with auto focus and a built-in flash, a video camera, an audio tape recorder, and pencil and paper, they set up camp on March 2, 2001, after the close of business. Before they officially began their investigation, one member of the group shivered as if a draft was blowing through that only he could feel. He explained to the others that the ghosts were doing 'walk-throughs,' whereby spirits pass through your body without stopping, causing full-body shudders and overall nerve tingling. That member has the ability to both see and hear spirit, and he noticed that a female spirit, dressed in red 1950s-style clothing was following a waitress around, seemingly interested in the employee's every move. Another member of the group later confirmed that spirit's description when she was again seen in the basement.

There was also a spirit interested in seeing the owner. He asked when Alex would arrive repeatedly, much like a child anticipating Santa's visit. With Alex as their host, the entire group headed to the basement. The basement is described as being

> " . . . constructed of cement block and built in such a way
> as to divide the space into two sections, one slightly
> larger than the other. While both sides provide storage for
> canned goods, dishes and other necessities, the larger side
> also has a wood construction storage room and a work-
> shop. The smaller side has a cage-type construction for
> storage. The washer, dryer, water heaters, etc. are located
> on the larger side, as are the stairs. The first thing you no-
> tice as you come down the stairs is that the storage room
> is not built against the outside wall. It was built a few feet
> away. The same is true of the workshop. The heating in
> the basement functions well, and the whole area is well
> lit. The area is well-maintained, and items that cannot be
> put on shelves are stacked on skids."

Alex told them that the basement was normally quite warm, but
they could all feel the chill that first night, a common indicator of the
presence of ghosts.

As expected, a spirit was immediately noticed standing in the
space between the outside wall and the storage room. It was a man of
average height with a beard, and he did not seem happy about the in-
trusion on his haunting grounds. A female member of the group of
investigators went to the area behind the storage room and unfortu-
nately met the same unhappy spirit head on. He shoved her in the
chest, causing pain and difficulty in catching her breath. He is the
only physically aggressive spirit at the diner, thankfully, and he
haunts only the basement.

Between the outside wall and the workshop, two of the more experienced members of the group found the air to be icy, even though
the heating duct just above their heads was blowing down warm air.
They quickly sensed two spirits in that spot. One had suffered a heart
attack (perhaps the big, beefy man with the black mustache who had
been seen by another psychic ten years earlier) and the other was the
aggressive spirit mentioned above. They now learned that he had

committed suicide, and he gave a clear message that was easily chan-neled: "I am very afraid. I do not want you here. This is my home." A little later, one member felt drawn back to the area, but when she turned to leave, she got the feeling that someone wanted her to stay. She then told the spirit that nobody was there to hurt him and he could take her hand and walk with her if he wanted to. According to their report, "She was actually a little surprised when he took her right hand and went for a walk. Another member of the group was able to confirm that, compared to her left hand, her right hand was icy." There was no further physical aggression from that particular spirit.

A flexible metal hoop used to clear the plumbing system lies on the smaller side of the base-ment. On this even-ing, the hoop had somehow twisted itself into a perfect figure eight when it was dropped. The figure eight is widely known as the infinity symbol, a never-ending circle of motion between the physical and spiritual planes; a symbol that tran-scends time and space. On the New Tarot, the infinity symbol depicts a man gazing through

Photo by Ron Guindon

Mysterious figure eight found in Spanky's base-ment.

death and being reborn. If they rigged the hoop to drop like a figure eight, the spirits could not have chosen a better symbol to portray their situation. Alex said there was no deliberate attempt to create such a symbol by himself or his employees.

At the end of their first evening, the group's members returned to the dining room to compare notes. The person in charge of videotaping the scene was disappointed to find that she was unable to keep the equipment in focus, even with its auto-focus feature. The most experienced member of the group, Ronnie Guindon, who is gifted with both psychic and artistic abilities, did a quick sketch of the faces he had seen in the basement. Several faces resemble the description provided by the two psychics in 1991. Ronnie was unaware of the earlier investigation and had never read their report.

One week later, several members of the original group returned to Spanky's to drop off copies of the photographs they had taken to Alex. While there, they made a short trip to the basement. Their report says, "There were not as many of us, and the spirits seemed a

Ron Guindon's sketch of spirits he encountered at Spanky's.

little more aggressive. One member reported being told telepathically to 'Get Out!' This time the basement was warm when we went down, and you could feel the cold swirl past you. One member stayed on the smaller side and, without realizing it, stood inside one end of the infinity hoop. The others went to the area by the workshop and, while they were there, she felt a rush of cold air pour toward her and stop in front of her, as if she were blocking it. Our most experienced member said the spirits were quite upset that night, and we left."

Undeterred, four members returned the following evening, March 10, planning to stay the entire night. Again, they waited for the staff to leave before heading back down into the basement—the hub of ghostly activity. The basement was warm, but they could feel cold air sweeping by and around them. The spirits were buzzing. One of the members of the group picked up on a conversation between two spirits who were commenting that their group of investigators seemed to be enjoying themselves. They then added that they were surprised that the eavesdropping member could hear their thoughts. The name of one of those spirits was Andrew.

This time Ronnie Guindon operated the video camera. The first time the group left the basement that night, he taped them going up the stairs and was following closely behind them. However, when he attempted to go up the stairs, the focus blurred on the camera, and he felt his way being blocked. On his second attempt to move forward, he was again blocked and got the impression that he was being forced to stay down there. Finally, on his third attempt to leave, he was allowed passage.

An audio tape recorder had been placed in the basement by two members who started it shortly after midnight. They hoped to capture the sound of spirit voices and ghostly activity, in a process known as Electronic Voice Phenomenon (EVP). The first recording proved to be inconclusive, so the recorder was repositioned in a different location. When the recorder was checked later, it was found with the pause button depressed, though the investigators are certain it was running properly when they left it. Again, no conclusive recordings were to be had. It was obvious the spirits were being difficult. When a member was sent to check on the tape recorder a third time, he felt his path blocked at the top of the stairs. Every nerve in his body tingled and the plastic covering the doorway seemed to tremble as he got the strong impression that someone was inaudibly telling him, "No. Not now."

Shortly afterwards, two different members of the group went into the basement with the video camera and the 35mm camera. First, they checked on the tape recorder, this time finding it situated behind an obstacle that had not been there previously. They knew they had not put it behind an obstacle and presumed that the obstacle must have been placed in the way of the recorder after they put it there, for the purpose of making it more difficult to get to. The tape was, however, still running, so they left it alone and continued on. While standing near the archway between the two sections of the basement, the video camera blurred out completely. They panned the area to be sure that they hadn't just been trying to focus on something too closely, but as they panned back toward the stairs, the focus again went out. They were beginning to feel like those whom they were investigating were investigating them. The hunter was becoming the hunted. Though they took photos at the time, those particular photos were not there when they had the film developed. They did, however, capture several blue orbs on film, as seen in the following photo. That, along with many other photos they got of speeding orbs, unexplained streaks and lights, and possible faces, offered physical proof that there was strong spirit activity in the basement at the time.

On their final trip to the basement, they finally met with some success when a member of the group was able to channel a spirit known as Abe. Abeneezer, as he was properly known, had been a preacher who had come to the area to work with the natives, and he died of fever. Abe said the other spirits were agitated by the presence of the investigators and did not want to talk to them. He explained he was not one of the diner's regular spirits, but came only because he had been called upon for help. The spirits, it seems, found the energy of the investigators to be disruptive to their work. Abe explained that the spirits who stayed there permanently were responsible for clean-

Photo by Ron Guindon
Orbs (balls of spirit energy) in basement of Spanky's.

ing up the negative energy on a continuing basis. He said, "We do not need any help. There are lots of things that you cannot see, and we are in one dimension while you are in another, and we should not interfere with each other."

None of Spanky's ghosts are a threat. They dwell within the basement and considerately wait until after hours to go about their business.

Plum Brook Milling Company

Russell

"Be he alive, or be he dead, I'll grind his bones to make my bread."
—Jack and the Beanstalk

They say that at midnight on a cool, crisp evening in the spring, if you pass by the hollow where an old flour mill once stood along Plum Brook in the Town of Russell, you can hear the creaking of the mill gate as it rises and the wheel begins to go around, as it grinds millstones, or perhaps bones, to dust. They say some have even seen the spectral image of a short, stoop-shouldered miller lifting a large container of something and pouring it into the hopper. They say that it's the ghost of Tom Shanley, replaying that fateful moment that would doom him to a life of infamy, shame, loneliness, and anonymity.

Mary Millington was a pretty, pleasant young woman of nineteen when she first befriended the much older Tom Shanley, an Englishman who had purchased the Plumb Brook Milling Company across the brook about a mile from where Mary lived with her widowed mother. The two women did his laundry and baked for him, and he in turn provided them with flour and bran for their services.

Not a lot was known about Shanley when he arrived in town, but it was believed that he brought his wealth from England and hid it somewhere in the mill. The elder Mrs. Millington, who lived by very modest means, was determined that Mary court the lonely miller, who had taken an instant liking to her, for her mother knew of the cache of gold pieces he had in his possession and only wanted a better life for her daughter. The matchmaking, however, may ultimately

79

have sealed her daughter's horrible fate.

Mary reluctantly allowed the widowed Shanley to woo her, but theirs was a doomed union, for their differences were many. He was more than twice her age. She was very lovely, but he was a short, club-footed cripple whose shoulders stooped as he hobbled about the mill, whose brows were furrowed into a permanent frown, and whose dark, beady eyes reflected all of the hate and bitterness he possessed within. Mary was friendly and outgoing, but Shanley was a loner who was bitter, obsessive, and vindictive. When a more appealing suitor in the form of George Ray, a handsome, young transient schoolmaster from Ohio, strode into town one day, Mary's attentions to the old miller were abruptly severed and given to Mr. Ray. This did not bode well with the vain old miller, who watched the new relationship develop before his very eyes. He became even more reclusive and more agitated by the day.

When school closed on March 16, 1862 for the last day of the school year, George Ray had hastily decided to enlist because of the war. After bidding a heart-broken Mary farewell, he headed out to find the nearest train station. A neighbor and a passing farmer, however, saw him that same evening, through the window of the schoolhouse he had taught at. They said it looked as if he was engaged in a heated argument with someone. It is not known why he went back to the schoolhouse, which still stands today, or whom he was arguing with. After that night, he was never seen again, and it was assumed that he had gone west to enlist, as planned.

The following evening, Mary told her mother that she would take a basket to Tom Shanley, because the bridge that connected their land to his had washed out, and all that was left were the stringer beams on which to cross. Mary would not have her mother trying to traverse the precarious structure, but she knew she herself could do it, as she had in the past. Her mother, secretly hopeful that Mary would take up her relationship with the miller again now that George Ray was gone, agreed to let her daughter go. That was the last time Mrs. Millington saw Mary. When her daughter didn't return that evening, she feared that Mary had fallen off the stringer beams into the swift-moving water below and been swept away. The next day, after new planks were laid across the bridge, she raced to the mill to see if Mary had been there, but the crusty old miller said he hadn't seen her and that she undoubtedly met up with George Ray at the schoolhouse and fled with him into the night. He refused to help search the small community for her, still so bitter was he that she had betrayed him.

At first, the people of the Plum Brook area considered that she might have ran off and eloped with Ray, as the miller had suggested. It then came out that a young country boy had gone to the mill for a bag of bran the night of Mary's disappearance and was brusquely ordered off the property by the miller, who the boy said was furiously stuffing wood into the box stove. The miller had been such a frightful sight that the boy ran away from the mill in terror. The next day, as the community searched for Mary, the mill was locked, but a young farmer passing by the mill at midnight heard the old mill gate lifted and the ominous whirring of the machine, and he could see Shanley emptying an ash sieve into the hopper. The focus of the disappearance of Mary Millington then turned toward Shanley, who the townspeople feared had vengefully killed her, burned her body in the great box stove and ground her bones to dust to destroy all evidence of her. The rumors even went so far as to suggest that George Ray had met the same fate as his ill-fortuned lover, at the hands of a jilted miller gone mad.

A Haunted Resort & Restaurant

Alexandria Bay

Chris has been a housekeeper at an elegant resort in Alexandria Bay for four years and an employee at a local restaurant, as well. Her job at the resort is to clean the offices, lounge, dining areas, lobby, and conference rooms, as well as a few cottages on the premises.

The first time she met a ghost was an experience she'll never forget. Every morning at the crack of dawn, Chris took her break in a booth on the second floor near the outside door in the lounge where she watched the sun come up. One morning when she was sitting there, across from the stairs, she thought she saw an arm outside the glass door out of the corner of her eye. As she turned her head to get a better look, she felt a whoosh of air and heard a loud crash all at once, as if someone had lunged at the push-type bar on the door very hard to open it. As you would expect in a story about ghosts, nobody else was in the lounge, or outside the door. She ran out to the front desk and breathlessly told the clerk what had happened, but the clerk was unconvinced.

When she went to work at the restaurant later that day, she told the story to her boss, Judy, whose father previously owned the resort—before he died. Judy explained that her father used to check up on his employees from time to time to make sure they weren't goofing off, and perhaps he was still there and devised a plan to get her up from her break and back to work. He had died, Judy continued, on the very stairs that Chris had been sitting across from that morning!

On another occasion, Chris was alone, vacuuming one of the resort's cottages, when she caught a glimpse of a woman standing on the stairs near the bottom of the staircase. She wore an old-fashioned white gown, had beautiful long hair, and was plainly visible for a few brief seconds before she vanished. Chris wasted no time informing the staff that she would not clean that room, unless someone stayed with her from then on. The bar staff obliged and never left until she was done cleaning. She later learned that the cottage had been a private home at one time, but doesn't have a clue as to the identity of the woman she saw.

Whenever Chris cleaned the upstairs offices, it always felt as if someone was right behind her or watching her, so she convinced the kind night auditor to go up there with her each night until she was done cleaning. One night when the night auditor was working down the hall from her, Chris was startled to hear banging on the wall beside her. It was loud enough that she could hear it plainly, even though she was listening to fairly loud music through her headset at the time. She thought the auditor was playing a joke on her, until she realized that two offices separated the women, and the auditor could not have raced back to her office before Chris ran out in the hall to see what was going on. The room where the banging emanated from was empty, not surprisingly. It seemed no matter where Chris went on the resort grounds, she would see things out of the corner of her eye that disappeared when she turned to face them. She could not escape the uneasy feeling of being followed as she went about her duties.

It was bad enough feeling stalked by an invisible presence at the resort, but when she found herself being watched by a different ghost at the restaurant, it was almost too much for Chris to bear. One day, as she was recounting her experiences at the resort to a coworker at the restaurant, she noticed a tall, dark-haired man wearing a dark turtleneck standing by the pool staring back at her. She thought it odd to be wearing a turtleneck in July. As the man stood with his arms crossed and the glorious Alexandria Bay sunset as his backdrop, Chris turned to ask her coworker if she knew who he was. Her coworker didn't see anyone standing there, and when Chris turned back, neither did she. He had vanished in the blink of an eye. Chris then described the man and was told that it sounded just like the restaurant's previous owner, who had died some time ago.

It seems that some people, like Chris, are more open to seeing spirit than others. To find out if you are such a person, why not plan your next vacation in the beautiful resort town of Alexandria Bay.

Haunted Halls

Plattsburgh

Around 1905 a grief-stricken janitor hanged himself in the basement of the impressive five-story New York State Normal & Training School in Plattsburgh, where the beautifully restored Hawkins Hall of SUNY Plattsburgh is located today. At the time, the man was living in the small caretaker's basement apartment of the brick, castle-like structure where he could ensure that the coal fires remained hot throughout the winter season. After all, he had about one hundred teachers-in-training and one hundred fifty young students, as well as the Normal School's faculty, to keep warm. But on that fateful day, he was too despondent over the recent death of his beloved wife to continue with his duties, or indeed his life.

Soon the school—which trained students to be teachers on the upper floors and had a model public school on the lower floors—began to take on a chill. A well-meaning third-grade teacher sent several of her pupils to the basement to inquire as to why the heat was not working, and there the youngsters found the man hanging. School closed for the day, and someone was asked to lower the flag to half-mast—a job the deceased man normally would have done. It was not long after that terrible day that some people claimed to see the janitor walking through the upper halls, as well as up on the roof ledge where the flagpole was, as if he were going about his usual routine. The sightings continued until 1929, when the Normal School burned to the ground in a devastating, still unexplained fire, but the legend lives on.

Hawkins Hall is the second oldest building (the oldest being the

Champlain Valley Hall, built in 1926) on the Plattsburgh college
campus. It was built in the early 1930s and was known then as the
new Normal Hall, which replaced the original Normal Hall after it
burned. In 1955, it was renamed in honor of George Hawkins, who
was principal of the teaching college for thirty-five years. Hawkins
Hall recently underwent a multi-million dollar renovation to restore it
to its original splendor, and then some. Looking up at the magnificent building today, it's hard to imagine the tragic events that took
place on that very site—first the suicide and then the fire—so many
years ago.

Photo by author
Plattsburgh State University's newly renovated Hawkins Hall.

Another Plattsburgh campus legend involves MacDonough Hall,
the third oldest building on the beautiful sprawling campus. Plans for
construction of MacDonough Hall began shortly after New York
State passed a law establishing the State University of New York
(SUNY) system in 1948. The hall, which served as Plattsburgh's first
college center and state-owned dormitory, was named after Commo-
dore Thomas MacDonough who led the American troops to victory
on Lake Champlain in 1814 during the final battle of the War of 1812.

Something unexpected occurred during excavation of the property that the hall now sits on. Two tombstones belonging to Plattsburgh's earliest white settlers—allegedly the first woman and the

first European child born in Plattsburgh—were discovered in a small, private burial plot on the marshy farmland. Obviously, they were in the way and would have to be moved. So, with the local newspaper on hand to report the historically significant find in the next day's paper, the stones were set by the side of the road, and the excavating continued. They didn't stay there long. By the following morning, the stones had come up missing—wouldn't you know—but it serves to add more drama to the legends of the ghosts of MacDonough Hall.

Photo by author

Plattsburgh State University's MacDonough Hall.

Students—at least twenty or thirty of them—have approached Douglas Skopp, SUNY Distinguished Teaching Professor of History at the college, begging for information on McDonough Hall that might shed some light on their own ghostly experiences. While Dr. Skopp doesn't necessarily believe in ghosts on campus, he does believe that the students are sincere in telling him that the lights flicker mysteriously, and they hear strange sounds or feel something unusual in the building. He attributes their experiences more to science than the paranormal, however. For example, lighting disturbances are probably just momentary electrical system glitches in the old building. Strange noises may be due to the many large windows or drafty doors leading to abandoned drainage tunnels that lead away from the basement. The tunnels were originally intended to provide underground access to other campus buildings, but when the building costs exceeded expectations, the tunnels were left unfinished.

Some students have reported hearing piano music coming from an empty room, seeing ghostly reflections in the mirrors, and hearing children crying or laughing or a woman screaming—her screech resounding throughout the entire building. One unconfirmed story is about a student who went snooping around the basement of the building one night and found his way to an old storage closet that was no longer used. When he opened the door, he saw two tombstones—*the* two missing tombstones—and when he heard a woman's voice behind him say that her grave should have been left alone, he promptly fainted. The only flaw with this story—just a minor detail really—is that the two grave markers are actually still missing. Details, details . . .

Then there is SUNY Plattsburgh's infamous "Mortimer the Ghost." What started as a very believable campfire ghost story told to incoming students during orientation in the late 1960s took on a life of its own, convincing many a trusting soul that a spirit named Mortimer haunts MacDonough Hall. Just who is this Mortimer guy? Dr. Skopp has no idea, and if anyone on campus did, it would be him. With his vast knowledge of the college's history, he has never run across the name anywhere. And if there's no Mortimer, then who *is* the male ghost many students have seen in MacDonough Hall over the years? Another unhappy spirit whose bones were dug up during construction?

Whether the mysterious Mortimer exists or not, here's a word to the wise: If you build on top of an old burial ground, you had better be prepared for just about anything—*especially* if you lose the gravestones!

The Musgrove Evans House

Chaumont

The Musgrove Evans House as it appears today.

The young child, pale and anemic, shakes uncontrollably in her bed. Her dangerously high fever causes recurring bouts of delirium, followed by grim periods of unconsciousness. This continues for several agonizing days, while the devout Quaker family prays in vain for the recovery of their daughter. On her final night, her breathing becomes labored and her palms turn bluish gray, as the Angel of Death takes hold of her tiny hands. They know he has come for her, just as he has come for so many of their neighbors in recent days.

(Summer of 1821, Jefferson County, NY)

91

In the 1820s, an epidemic of swamp fever, or ague, swept through the newly formed community of Chaumont in Jefferson County. Before it had subsided, many who survived the deadly virus had moved on to more hospitable land in other regions of the burgeoning country. Musgrove Evans, for whom Evan's Mills is named, was one. In 1818, he came to Jefferson County from Philadelphia, Pennsylvania, as a land agent and surveyor for the French landowner and developer, James D. LeRay de Chaumont. Several Quaker families accompanied him to the area, and together they settled on a 370-acre farm where Mr. Evans built a large limestone house—the house this story is about. An early "mover and shaker" of the community, he served as the town's second postmaster from 1818 to 1823, before moving on to Michigan with his wife Abi and their five young children and founding the town of Tecumseh. The other Quaker families had left the area prior to him, eager to escape the land that supplied both the dreaded virus and the ground in which to bury its unfortunate victims.

Today, Ronald and Diane Kines own the old stone house that Evans and his fellow Quakers built. It sits on a small hill on County Route 179 where Evans Street branches off to Depauville in the village of Chaumont. They have experienced their share of ghostly phenomena in the house and have learned first-hand that the spirits in residence are many and varied.

One is thought to be Philip Gaige, a prominent early citizen of Lyme and Chaumont who, along with his father John, purchased the home from Musgrove Evans. Mr. Gaige, following in Evans footsteps, served as Chaumont's postmaster for a total of nine years and as the Town of Lyme supervisor for three years. His likeness once appeared in an upstairs hall mirror to a young child and to the Kines' stunned daughter-in-law, on her first visit to the home. The image remained in the mirror for several moments, which was time enough for the incredulous woman to spin around and establish that someone hadn't come up from behind her in the hallway. The next day the same lady came upon a small oval portrait that adorned the wall behind a door in the library. She gasped. It was none other than Mr.

Gaige, the man she had seen in the mirror!

The spirits of Roy and Jessie Burlingame appear to be fonder of their former home than they were to each other in life. In 1922 Mrs. Burlingame shot and killed her husband, then turned the gun on herself, in an apparent fit of rage or despair. Nobody knows why the double homicide took place that summer day, but some have suggested that Jessie found out about Roy's infidelity or Roy found out about Jessie's adultery and threatened to leave her. Others have said she became enraged because Roy stayed out late that Saturday night when she wasn't feeling well. When he returned home, she shot him several times, then aimed the gun at her heart and fired. Perhaps it was a combination of theories; nobody will ever know. He was forty-three and she was thirty-one. The ill-fated pair may be responsible for some of the unexplained odors that have permeated the residence. Mrs. Kines has noticed a very strong flowery perfume of unknown origin in her home on various occasions, and Mr. Kines has smelled what he believes are expensive and imported cigars, but has never seen the smoke that would accompany them. For a home that does not allow smoking, it's also very strange that several members of the family have detected a sweet tobacco scent in the living room.

The Kines' oldest daughter saw a ghost in the basement nearly twenty-five years ago when she was in her early twenties and her grandfather owned the home. He had sent her to fetch something in the basement, and when she went down, she was horrified to see a man standing in the corner, wearing a straw hat and overalls. She raced upstairs and urged her grandfather to go see who it was, but by then the spirit had vanished. To this day, the daughter still has not returned to the basement.

At least one spirit in the home is able to move objects, as their son discovered firsthand. The teenager was lying in bed in an upstairs bedroom one night when a tabletop mirror across the room tipped over. He got up out of bed and put it back in its proper position. Just as he sat back down on the bed, the mirror went down again; and again the confused youngster got up, walked across the room, and stood it back up. At that very moment, a heavy chunk of ceiling plaster fell on the bed in the exact spot where he had been sitting. Thanks to a concerned ghost, he had been "sent" to the other side of the room and was spared from harm. Maybe it was the spirit of Philip Gaige who seems to have a fondness for mirrors, as previously mentioned.

Cats are innately mysterious creatures, especially the ghostly ones associated with this story. One was seen walking right through closed doors in the Kines home by one of their children. Others have been spotted in the windows by neighbors and family members, even though the Kines have no cats, and neither did Mrs. Kines' parents who were the previous owners. A thoughtful paperboy once set a cat back indoors when it came out as he was putting the paper inside. When the owners came home, as usual, there were no signs of the feline intruder.

Mr. and Mrs. Kines are not at all bothered by their haunted abode. In fact, they say it keeps things interesting—and it invariably comes up in conversation at family gatherings.

A Father and Daughter's Story

Carthage

Tiffany has always been sensitive to the spirit world. From a very young age, she got the tingly feelings of being watched when she was alone in empty rooms. It first happened in her grandfather's home on Route 11, just south of Adams, when she lived there with her mother, grandfather, and siblings. Her mother casually suggested that it was probably her deceased grandmother checking up on her. Her father agreed, telling her not to worry, because whoever it was would never hurt her. A "daddy's girl" through and through, she was comforted by his words, and they helped form the foundation of her beliefs regarding spirits, even though she would learn that there are exceptions to every rule.

Nobody could convince her, for example, that it was her grandmother's voice or a harmless spirit that she heard in the attic one day in 1996. Her mother sent her upstairs to see if her brother had turned off the radio and lights, since he was at work. She was about to shut off his radio, when she heard three loud bangs from the other side of the big red door in his room that led to the attic. Then someone yelled, "Let me out!" in a deep, scary voice. Terrified and sobbing, she raced downstairs and told her mother and grandfather. They were unable to dispel her fears, and she never went up there alone again. In a couple years, she would move in with her father.

Solomon Young built the 130-year-old farmhouse where Tiffany lives today with her father, Kevin. The house is on a dirt road called the Youngs Mills Road outside of Carthage. Kevin's grandparents bought it from Mr. Young and passed it down to his parents. Kevin then inherited it from his parents when they passed away. His father died in 1989 when he was eighty-six and his mother died in 1998 when she was ninety-four, but they have been back occasionally to check up on things.

Kevin returned to work as a mechanic at Fort Drum the week after his mother's funeral. While standing beside his toolbox his first day back, he noticed a very strong smell of plants; admittedly, not an odor generally associated with mechanics. It smelled just like it did at the wake and the funeral, and it lasted about five minutes. At about the same time, Tiffany was at school at South Jefferson when she smelled it at her locker and then again in class. Again, the smell lasted several moments before fading. When Kevin learned that his brother had also smelled flowers where he worked the same week, they both figured their mother had been checking on them, making sure they were getting on with their lives okay.

A couple of years later, Kevin awoke to the smell of his mother's home-cooked breakfast of bacon, eggs, toast and coffee. Once fully alert, he decided his daughter must have been up making breakfast, but she was still sleeping. It was eight o'clock, the same time his mother always had breakfast ready when she was alive. When Tiffany woke up a little later, she distinctly smelled toast and strawberry jam, but she knew it wasn't her father making it, because he had already left for work. Only the two of them live there now, so if neither made any of the things they smelled, who did?

Not to be outdone by his wife's flair for emitting memory-evoking aromas from beyond the grave, the spirit of Kevin's father Milt, who died in 1989, tried his hand at the same thing last year. Kevin explained, "We no longer have any farm animals, except for a few geese, three dogs and three cats. If you've ever been on a farm, you know the different smells of the animals and the manure smell that remains on you and your clothes after you leave the barn. In the house there was a particular chair located in the living room by the kitchen door that Dad used to sit in when he came in from the barn. Last year as I sat by the kitchen door, I got the strong smell of the cow barn and the smell of Dad's barn coat from so many years ago."

96

Even more impressive than the odor recall was Milt's ability to move fixed objects from his dimension. Anyone who has seen the hit movie, "Ghost," can appreciate how difficult this ability must be for a spirit to master. In 1996 Kevin's mother was bedridden with a broken hip. Kevin was carrying a pile of folded laundry into her room one day when three of his father's ball caps "jumped off the vanity" as he walked by them. Thinking it might have just been a loose floorboard causing the vanity to jiggle and the hats to bounce off, he came back into the room again and walked by the dresser exactly the same way as he had the first time, but nothing happened. Any doubts he had about whether the caps came off the dresser on purpose, were dismissed a few weeks later when he entered the room where his mother lay only to have the caps literally hurled off the dresser by an unseen hand as he walked by it. He is convinced it was his father's spirit, testing more of his ghostly abilities.

Tiffany sensed a presence in the kitchen one night when she was having dinner with her father and grandmother. When she got up to go to the fridge, she stepped right into a cold spot beside her grandmother. It felt like it was a freezer, but she had not yet reached the refrigerator. With her next step, she was back into normal room temperature. On her return, she again walked through the cold spot beside her grandmother, and back into normal room temperature. Later that evening her grandmother, who was ninety-one at the time, asked where Milt (her late husband) was. Kevin delicately explained that he wasn't with them anymore, but the spunky old woman replied, "Well, he was there at dinnertime." Had his spirit been standing behind her creating the cold spot that Tiffany walked through? When Tiffany heard her grandmother say that, she got chills down her spine, and this time it wasn't because of the sudden, unexplained drop in room temperature.

While Milt has certainly pulled off some attention-grabbing stunts since he died, he can be subtler. An outdoorsman and a hunter in his younger days, he had owned his share of guns and had traded them or sold them when money was tight. He enjoyed describing his old guns to Kevin, who was also a gun enthusiast and collector. At one gun show in Clayton in 1994, Kevin bought an impressive old Swiss army rifle with a checkered stock. Once he got home, he eagerly looked his latest acquisition over, noting all the little details, when he realized that he *knew* this gun. He started to recall all that his father had told him of just such a gun. His father had told him of the barrel that he had shortened and the 1918 coin he attached to it as a front site. Even the piece of old shoe leather his father had stuffed inside of the worn shell carrier pinhole to fill in the space was still intact. After all those years, he had been led to his father's old gun, and now he plans to keep it in the family.

Some incidents have occurred in their home that can't be as easily ascribed to Kevin's late parents; in fact, some occurred while they were still alive. When Kevin's niece was using the spare bedroom

Two cats with company (note the orb hovering overhead).

during a visit one time, she looked out the window and saw a blue sphere across the road from the house that came quickly through the meadow and then continued on down the road. Similarly, Kevin's parents told him of seeing a blue light float across their bedroom one night before disappearing into the living room where its light flooded the whole room. The blue sphere and light may have been orbs— balls of spirit energy in their purest form. Photographs are now regularly taken of such phenomena.

Kevin and Tiffany both have heard doors slamming in the evening. It has always happened around seven o'clock as they sat around the living room watching television, and there was never any explanation for the noise when they went to investigate. Kevin knows it wasn't the wind, because whenever he went to check, everything fell silent and the door was always closed securely. It sounded like their woodshed door opening and slamming shut, right down to the scraping sound the door made along the cement floor. The noises continued until the door was changed when they had their house remodeled.

Other unexplained sounds and noises have mystified the two in recent years. Kevin once heard the sound of a car approaching when he was working across the creek near his home. The sound was so clear that he could even hear the car stop, the car doors shut, and people's voices. He expected them to hear him hammering and head toward him. However, he soon heard the car doors close, the engine start up, and the car pull away and head back down the road from where it came. That made him a little more than curious, because he was sure they had to know he was there. So he got up and went to take a look. No car was in sight heading down the road, no dust from the dirt road was settling in the hot summer air, and no tracks were apparent in the gravel driveway. Fresh tracks were always easy to disseminate in their driveway, and the fact that there were none made him wonder if he had heard a ghost car. He knew of a woman from Lowville whose dead parents returned in a car to visit her, and when they left, they drove the car down the street where it vanished into thin air.

A car came into play in another mysterious incident at their home a year after his mother passed away, when his sister stopped by to sort through their mother's clothes and belongings. She asked Kevin to carry some boxes out to load into her car while she put away the rest of the items. When he got to the car, however, he found the doors locked and the keys in the ignition, so he set the boxes on the trunk and returned to the house. His sister was surprised and denied with great certainty locking the doors herself when she got out of the car.

Tiffany has had some pretty perplexing experiences herself. One day when she was eleven, she was playing alone in her room with a Ouija board that her father had had since he was a child. She was surprised to discover that it was working, even without the usual number of participants. But she was feeling brave and curious, so she asked whomever she was talking to from "the other side" if they would be there when she turned around. The answer was yes; but when she looked over her shoulder, there was nothing. She then asked if they were attached to the board, and they said yes. Still she saw no sign of anything unusual anywhere in the room, so she put the board back in its box and forgot about it, assuming it hadn't worked. Later that evening when she was about to shower, she heard the closet door in the bathroom creak open. Yet when she looked over at it, she saw that it was shut tight. Then while she was washing her hair in the shower, she heard the loud bang of the toilet seat slamming shut. Quickly rinsing the soap from her eyes, she peaked out of the tub but found nothing again. Not caring that suds were still in her hair, she jumped out of the shower, got dressed and ran to bed with her grandmother. She has never touched a Ouija board since.

I wonder if an undesirable spirit took the opportunity to invade their home on that night. If so, it could explain the presence that Kevin saw in the washroom only a year ago. He glanced up as he was putting on his shoes and saw a black, shadowy figure pass by the doorway. It was moving from the kitchen toward the front door very quickly, almost superhumanly. The frightening presence seemed like someone well over six feet tall wearing a black cloak with a hood over the head. It was the closest thing to an apparition that Kevin has seen, but it was quite close enough.

Tiffany recalls a time in 1999 when she had just woken up and her father was at work. As usual, she turned her radio on with the volume low when she heard the front door open and a man's voice yell, "Hello!" She quickly shut off her radio and ran to the window, only to find the driveway empty. Garnering her courage to go downstairs and investigate, she stood at the top of the stairs listening intently, and hesitating, for at least five minutes. Finally, she went downstairs and looked around. Luckily, no intruder was to be found, but strangely enough, the door was still locked.

Last summer Tiffany was playing basketball in the driveway, while her father was gone on a walk, when she heard voices coming from inside the house. Thinking it must be the radio, she checked it when she went back in but found that it was turned off. She never did figure out who or what it was that she heard on those two occasions.

Unexplained footsteps have been heard, as well, on the stairs in the house. Kevin had been asleep for an hour or so when Tiffany and a friend who was spending the night heard someone walking up the creaky old steps several months ago. Tiffany tried to calm her frightened friend, but the girl was not in the least convinced that the noise was nothing.

Kevin and Tiffany are used to the ghostly antics in their home and find it easy to believe in the spirit world that so obviously surrounds them. There is never a dull moment in their lives, and while there are occasionally unexplainable incidents, it's a comfort for them to realize that the spirits of their loved ones watch over them still.

Going Nowhere Fast

Watertown

It happened in the winter of 1975. Randy Besio was a college student living in a tiny apartment near Holcomb and Paddock Streets in the city of Watertown. He couldn't explain it then, and he can't explain it now. But the memory is as vivid as the day it occurred. Not many people forget the first time they met a ghost.

His one-room apartment in the sprawling L-shaped Victorian-style mansion was on the second floor. The imposing white structure reminded Randy of a southern plantation home. Holcomb and Paddock streets were lined with such homes, historical and elegant, at least in their glory days. But the homes had, since their creation in the mid-1800s, been heavily remodeled, leaving little semblance to what they had once been. This particular building, for example, was partitioned into eighteen small apartments. *Eighteen!* There were hallways leading to nowhere. It was a mystery, and a shame, that anyone would turn such a magnificent building into so many little, unimpressive apartments.

One cold night, more than a year after moving into the building, Randy rushed home from a night class to drop off some books and get changed to go out with some friends. It was snowing lightly, and he automatically tapped the snow off his shoes as he came through the back door, so he wouldn't lose his footing on the hardwood floors. Funny thing was, the door didn't make the telltale sound of clicking shut behind him that he was so used to. Maybe it was sticking or sluggish. The landlord would want to know, because he was a stickler for saving energy. He loved to remind the tenants that it cost

103

money to heat the stairway. As he rounded the first bend in the stairs, Randy was surprised that the door had still not shut like it usually did. He'd be sure it was secured on his way out. Approaching the second landing, he noticed the sound of footsteps behind him. That explained it. He hadn't heard the door shut because someone had come in right behind him. Strange that he hadn't seen anyone. When he reached the second floor and went to unlock his apartment door, he paused to see who had been behind him. The steps continued, reached the second floor landing, and then headed straight toward Randy. How could that be? There was nobody there, and yet, the sounds of footsteps were getting louder and closer. Suddenly, he felt something brush past him and could hear it continue down the hallway where it turned left, but whatever it was didn't take the turn in the hallway. The noise stopped right at the wall where the hallway turns left, as if it had gone straight through the wall and into another tenant's apartment.

Completely taken aback, Randy could barely manage to turn the key to open his door, and when he did, he merely tossed the books on the floor, turned, and rushed back downstairs. The back door was now latched, like it should be—but like it wasn't just moments before—and when he opened it, he noted that there was only one set of footprints—his—in the fresh snow. Whoever it was that was in such a hurry to go nowhere upstairs was either floating or weightless. And what's more, they were invisible!

Could it have been just the usual creaking and settling of an old house? Randy had been there long enough to be familiar with all the little noises the house could make, and this wasn't one of them. Neither was the sound of someone clearly whispering his name in his ear one night as he lay down to sleep, effectively producing an instant and prolonged state of insomnia in the poor man.

Nonetheless, Randy continued living in the house for another year or so after his unexplained encounters, before moving to Massena where he now lives. He can't help but wonder if anyone else has ever heard the mysterious footsteps or felt the strange rush of air passing by in the hallway. I'd be willing to bet they have.

Burrville Cider Mill

Burrville

Burrville Cider mill as it appears today.

The Burrville Cider Mill, one of the oldest establishments in Jefferson County, is a family business now owned and operated by Gregory and Cynthia Steiner, Sr. and Tina and Gregory Steiner, Jr. When it was first constructed at the bottom of a thirty-foot waterfall on the North Branch of Sandy Creek in 1801, it was known as Burr's Mills and was used as a sawmill and a gristmill, neither of which remains today. The Steiners purchased the property in 1996 and had been forewarned that it had a haunted history but were undaunted.

After all, they had cider to press, fresh cider doughnuts to fry, and a booming business to tend to. There would be no rest for the weary in this establishment and no rest for the dead, either, as they would soon learn. Before long a ghostly odd couple lovingly referred to as Homer and Captain Burr began clamoring for their attention.

Homer is a good ghost—helpful, obedient, hard working and dependable. He was Homer Rebb, and he can be credited with turning the mill into a commercial business when he owned it in the 1940s. Burr would be Captain John Burr, the mysterious pirate who bought the year-old mill in 1802 and for whom both the mill and the town are named. Captain Burr is the opposite of Homer. Even shadier since he became a ghost, he's an old swindler who hasn't changed much in 200 years! Rumor has it that in his day he stole from ships on Lake Ontario, and then sold the goods to troops in Sackets Harbor. He's still up to his old tricks.

Tools and other items sometimes turn up missing, the largest being a twenty-five-pound bag of sugar. Tina Steiner clearly recalls putting the bag in the back room at the end of the day, then locking the door and going home. The next morning she was the first one to open up, and when she went to retrieve the sugar from the back room, she found that the bag was missing, but nothing else was disturbed. The sugar has still never been found. A cordless drill also came up missing one day, but by the time Tina had asked around to see who might have taken it, it mysteriously reappeared in the very spot it had vanished from just moments before. Elementary ghost behavior, and no doubt the doings of Captain Burr.

Captain Burr is probably also responsible for making all the noise in the attic, playing his rowdy pirate part to the hilt. Basically, all that's up there are a number of empty plastic jugs, yet the sound of heavy objects dropping on the attic floor is often heard. Whenever anyone has gone to investigate, nothing has been found amiss, and the light jugs have always remained in their upright positions. Other mysterious noises have been heard in the building, as well. Cindy Steiner once clearly heard the sound of a ping-pong ball bouncing across the floor in the store area when she was alone, but she was never able to find the source for that sound. She and the others have also heard the grating sound of an old double cider press in the basement when nobody is down there, as if the metal wheels are turning themselves on their metal track.

Homer, who was always dressed properly in a suit and tie when he was alive, gets the credit for fixing things and keeping a watchful eye over the place. Whenever equipment fails for no apparent reason, Tina and Cindy ask, "Homer, will you fix it?" and the cooperative ghost gets it going right away. He probably is also the one who shows up in the kitchen when the women are doing dishes. Both Tina and Cindy have noticed a ghostly presence when they have been alone in the room. The cabinets open and shut behind their backs, but if the women simply say, "Homer, go home," the strange behavior stops.

One time Cindy propped the cooler door open so she could fill it, and the glass fogged up because it was such a hot, muggy day. As she went about her business, she felt that she was being watched. She hadn't heard anyone come in, because the fans were on, and they would have masked the noise. But she could sense that she wasn't alone, so she jokingly said, "Hello, Captain Burr," as if to casually greet the resident ghost. That was when she saw a man, or at least a part of him. Showing in the reflection of the opened cooler door, as if he were standing behind her, she saw a his legs and feet. He was wearing heavy black hunting-type pants made of wool and brown leather work boots. She spun around to see who it was, but nobody was there. Cindy was the only one in the building, and the parking lot was empty. Obviously, no living customer would've been wearing heavy wool pants and boots on such a hot and humid day. Cindy doesn't believe it was the ghost of Homer, because he never dressed that way; so it must have been the elusive Captain Burr.

One of the ghosts, probably Captain Burr, has a penchant for big old stogies. A cigar that was covered with cobwebs was once found lying in a newly cleaned and painted spot, though nobody has ever been seen smoking that type of cigar in the building. Tina and Cindy and some of the employees have smelled cigar smoke in the sorting room, under the kitchen sink, in a confined area of the store, and in the parking lot. Every time, the smell only lasted for only a few seconds. One time Cindy was driving along on her way home when she suddenly smelled cigar smoke so strongly that it stung the inside of her nose. The odor had dissipated by the time she got home, but it had been so powerful that she asked everyone if they could still smell it on her clothes. It's pretty likely that Captain Burr hitched a ride that night.

Things occasionally get knocked off the walls by unseen hands—one day it happened a record five different times—but Cindy caught the invisible culprit in the act when two candles went down off the shelf right before her eyes. There was no breeze in the store that day, and the earth wasn't shaking from some rare earthquake in these parts or a big truck going by. There was simply no reason for a sturdy box holding two candles to suddenly drop from the shelf to the floor, especially when they were at least a good six inches from the edge of the shelf; but then, this is a story about ghosts, so what would you expect?

Cindy's sister, Judy, was working at the cash register one day when she noticed a piece of candy that is sold at the Mill on the floor under a display unit. She picked it up, but then later in the day, several times, she found it back on the floor—always the same color candy and always pointing in the same direction. Another employee was jugging cider in the jugging room one time when the lights went off and back on. It was the only room affected by the momentary blackout. He assumed someone was playing a joke on him, and was a little unnerved to learn that nobody was responsible—no *living* body, that is.

Whether the ghosts at the Burrville Cider Mill are actually Homer and Captain Burr may never be known for sure, but they are harmless and usually pretty accommodating. One night when a television film crew was visiting the grounds to film some footage for their Halloween special, for example, an outdoor light flickered where they stood, much to everyone's delight. Since this was a motion detector light, Cindy wasn't surprised to see the light go on, because some critter could have set it off; but when it flickered on and off constantly during the interview, she knew it must be their ghost. Two members of the film crew did not believe in ghosts prior to visiting the mill, but after the above incident and their interviews with the Steiners, they've now joined the ranks of believers.

Cindy admits that she came right out and told the ghosts the night before opening day that she had a right to be there as much as they did, and they would get along just fine as long as they never scared her. She went even further that night and asked them for proof that they even existed. They had just replaced the kitchen floor where an old piece of tin had covered the rotted wood, and she was putting sealer on the new tile. So while she was getting all of her thoughts and concerns aired for any ghosts who might be listening, she dared them to leave a single footprint in the fresh sealer during the night. Unbeknownst to Cindy, her son Greg Jr. was working on a truck after she had left and locked up, and he needed something from the mill, so he let himself in and took *one step* onto the kitchen floor when he realized it had just been waxed and sealed. He quickly backed off. The next morning when Cindy arrived, she went to the kitchen, not really expecting to find the requested footprint from their ghost. She nearly keeled over when she saw the single footprint. Greg Jr. noticed her shock and thought it was because she was upset that he had accidentally stepped on the floor, so he apologized profusely until Cindy told him what she had asked the ghost to do. As far as she is concerned, she got her proof—even if it wasn't from the ghost itself. She reasons that maybe the ghost somehow psychically led Greg Jr. to the kitchen where he proceeded to impress the floor with a single footprint. It's a story they all chuckle about now. Of course, since that first opening day, they've been provided with much more proof that the mill is, indeed, truly haunted.

The mill, which has become a tradition for many local families to visit each autumn, sells cider, homemade baked goods and fudge, apples, Indian corn, crafts, cheese curd, and more. You can also view the falls that offer a backdrop to the mill. If you would like to visit, they are open seven days a week from 9 A.M. until 8 P.M., Memorial

Day through Thanksgiving Eve. They are located in Burrville about five minutes southeast of Watertown off Route 12 at 18176 County Route 156 (Plank Road). You can also visit them on the web at www. burrvillecidermill.com.

Ruby's Castle

Watertown

You are my haven.
Never alone.
Forever sheltering life.
You will always be my home.
                              — Ruby

Ruby was too excited about moving into the large old Victorian—clearly the most splendid home on the street—to give it a second thought when she discovered sixteen silver crucifixes and thirteen Italian horns positioned just so in the basement and dried sage bundles stylishly hung throughout the rest of the house like something out of *Better Homes & Gardens*. Some time later, once things had settled down a bit, she learned that Italian horns are worn about the neck to ward off the dreaded "evil eye," and that sage is an herb commonly used in the blessing and cleansing of homes. Maybe the previous owner wouldn't tell her everything about the home or its history, but Time would certainly tell.

It wasn't long before echoes of history reverberated throughout the halls of her new home, waking Ruby from a sound sleep and drawing her toward the source. She heard a baby crying, and while she knew it was impossible—she had no babies in her home—she found her way to the very room from which the sound emanated, and then it was gone. A guest who had been staying in the home with her finally moved to a bedroom downstairs after breaking down and admitting that she, too, had heard a baby crying. Ruby began to research the history of her home and learned that a baby and a toddler had died in the home in 1889. They were both buried in the nearby Brookside Cemetery. And there were other interesting stories associated with the old house, as well.

It seems a woman went insane in the home and was carried out kicking and screaming and taken to a sanitarium. Maybe it was her footsteps that another guest to the home swears she heard one night. Or maybe it's her spirit that talks to Ruby's young granddaughter, prompting the four-year-old to make uncharacteristically adult-like comments when her grandmother asks her who she's whispering to. Then again, her granddaughter's invisible companion might also be a young girl whose apparition was caught on web cam as she leaned over a family friend who was sitting on the couch.

Another visitor to the home once announced, "This house has voices." He then went on to say that he continually heard someone singing a song that referred to Ruby's name. Even the family pets—especially the family pets, in fact—are sensitive to the many entities in the home, and they don't like what they can't see anymore than their human companions do! Two dogs had to be given away when it became apparent that their constant barking and fur-raising growls were a result of being too spooked to continue living there. The two resident cats also growl often at things nobody else can see, but they seem to be okay if they stay only on the first floor.

The most disturbing event occurred very recently. Ruby was lying in bed and noticed a large man out at the street corner walking towards her house making the sign of the cross and praying. His gait picked up speed until he was trotting, then running past her window, all the while screaming. He frantically rang the doorbell and, in hysterics, he blurted out, "There's a man in your tower hanging himself!" He demanded to know who it was. Ruby, at a loss for words and not so sure this guy was playing with a full deck, said, "You tell me!" With that, the hysterical man ran back out to the street, looked up at the tower, and called out, "Who are you?" Then he came running back to the house and gave Ruby a man's name—the very name of a previous owner. Ruby called the police, not just because she had a hysterical stranger at her door, but also because she didn't know what—if anything—was going on up in her attic, and then she ran to the attic door. She had been up there many times, but this time it was bone-biting cold in front of the door. She hesitated for a moment before opening the door but wasted no time slamming it shut again, for inside was an eerie red glow. Her scientific mind could not explain away a light of that nature, or the sudden chill around the door, and she has never been back up to the tower since.

The woman Ruby bought the home from enlightened her—better late than never—about another event that occurred in the house's history. Another previous owner actually did hang himself from the tower. He broke out one of the tower windows, tied a rope around his neck, and jumped out of the tower so that everyone could witness his final act. His name was, indeed, the name that the incoherent stranger had provided when he told Ruby there was a man in her tower.

As for Ruby, she loves her home, spirits and all, and has no plans to leave. Something about the house draws people in and makes them want to stay forever. Evidently many of them do just that!

Murder in the Harbor

Sackets Harbor

Shortly after he was born, Ivan's parents moved into a quaint old house just off Main Street in the picturesque village of Sackets Harbor. Their enviable waterfront property boasted a spectacular view of Lake Ontario, with the backyard overlooking the harbor. While his father was away at work in those first days, his mother, Jean, set about the task of unpacking and making their house feel like home. It should have been a wonderful, exciting time, but there was something—or someone—who would not let her enjoy this time in her life, and she wouldn't fully understand why for more than twenty years.

Almost immediately, Jean noticed something amiss. It wasn't anything in her physical surroundings; it was something intangible—a feeling of being watched by an invisible intruder who was so close to her that his icy breath sent chills down her spine and made the hair on the back of her neck stand up. For weeks it got worse every time she tried to organize their belongings in the upstairs back room overlooking the lake. The fear she felt in that room and in the front upstairs bedroom was often so strong that she would be overcome with the urge to get out and run downstairs.

Ivan's father didn't want to even consider what his wife told him she was experiencing. He believed that *she* believed it, but he didn't feel it was actually occurring. He simply didn't believe in all that stuff. She knew she would have to get to the bottom of it by herself.

When she visited the people they had bought the house from and asked if they'd ever experienced anything unusual in the house, they abruptly ended the conversation and closed the door, leaving her

115

standing alone on the porch stunned. By not answering, they had inadvertently given her their answer, however, and it was just as she had thought. Yes. But the confirmation that someone other than herself had experienced something disturbing in the house was not enough to resolve the situation, so she visited her minister and asked him to bless the house. The insensitive pastor bluntly responded that if she felt so badly about the house, then she "should just move." Another door closed in her face. Jean returned home dejected.

Ivan's sister was just two years old when she first told her mother about the nice person who talked to her at night in the room she shared upstairs with Ivan. Unlike the feelings of dread that Jean got when she sensed the spirit nearby, the little girl felt no malevolence from the mysterious stranger, so the fear didn't consume her like it did her mother. Maybe it wasn't even the same spirit, or maybe children just accept communication with the spirit world as normal, until society convinces them otherwise.

Three-year-old Ivan, meanwhile, was having a very vivid, recurring bad dream that continued until he was five or so. He kept the odd dream to himself, forgetting about it until he was an adult. This was his dream:

"The dream would start with me looking out of the upstairs window down at the yard below. Out beyond the yard, there were gray storm clouds over the lake, and the water was choppy. If you've ever seen a storm come into Sackets Harbor, you know how ferocious the sky can look! There, below in the yard, I would see a silver steel tub full of water. In the water was a young boy, and above him stood a man. The man was very angry, and he was holding the boy completely under the water, strangling him and drowning him all at once. The boy was struggling to break free as the man held him under. Water was sloshing around. I would then suddenly see this awful scene as though I was standing in the yard about ten feet behind the man's right shoulder. Then, suddenly I would see everything as though *I* was the one underwater and the man was drowning *me*. He was a terrible man, and I can remember impressions of his grin, though not really any other details of his face. That was the whole dream. It was the same each time, and it went on for a few years. I was maybe four at the time they peaked."

What could make a young boy have such a persistent horrible dream? Dream analysts would say that recurring dreams occur when the dreamer is not getting the message the subconscious or higher conscious is sending to them through symbolic elements in the dream. The more important the dream is for the dreamer to interpret and understand, the more persistently the dream will recur. However, it is becoming more widely accepted today in spiritual and metaphysical circles that dream messages can come, not only from our own subconscious, but also from the spirit world. In Ivan's case, many years later, long after the recurring dreams had ceased, he would come to believe that the strange dream had come from a distressed spirit, trapped in the shadow lands between Heaven and Earth.

Ivan's father was the last to experience something out of the ordinary in the house. It made the skeptic an instant believer in ghosts. He and his wife were sleeping in a downstairs bedroom that had been added onto the original house many years before. The room was always cold, even though new insulation had been added. That fact alone often raises a red flag for paranormal investigators, but the vast majority of people would dismiss such an anomaly, convincing themselves that they simply have a stubborn draft or anything that is more believable than a ghost in residence!

"One night," Ivan said, "my mother was startled out of her sleep to see a glowing figure walking towards her side of the bed. A yellowish light surrounded it. As it got closer, she was able to make out more distinct features. It appeared to be a young boy with dingy blonde hair wearing a hooded, green sweatshirt. As he came closer she realized, to her horror, that he was angry! She was paralyzed with fear when he came up to her and got right in her face. At that moment, she screamed and jumped on top of my father, who also saw the apparition just as it vanished."

The sense of being watched and followed in the house diminished after that incident, but other, more substantial things began happening. Furniture moved on its own, like the rocking chair rocking itself. Objects slid across tables. Footsteps could be heard upstairs when nobody was up there.

Unable to get the ghostly image of the angry boy out of her mind, and certain that he had been trying to tell her something, Jean asked her mother to try to find out if anyone knew anything about the house's history. Finally, Ivan's grandmother was able to shed considerable light on the situation. Apparently, a single mother and her young son had once occupied the house they lived in. The mother became involved with a sailor who had come to port in the harbor and struck up a relationship with her. They eventually moved in together, but the man never got along with her son. One day he took the boy out in a silver boat to supposedly go fishing on the lake. A newspaper article she found stated that the boy had drowned. The man, however, had made it back to shore to give a one-sided explanation as to the boy's accidental drowning.

Remember Ivan's dream of an angry man strangling a young boy in choppy waters out back of their house? He had those alarming dreams nearly twenty years *before* he knew anything about what his mother had experienced in the house or what his grandmother discovered from the newspaper article. At the time, they understandably didn't want to alarm the children with speculation. So Ivan had no knowledge of the boy who drowned until he was twenty-two years old, and Jean was telling him about their "old, haunted house in Sackets Harbor," as they sat around the kitchen table chatting one night. In his dream, the choppy waters in the shiny silver tub in the backyard may have represented the rough waters of the stormy harbor and a silver aluminum fishing boat, commonly used by the locals. All the other scenes from his dream could very well have been meant literally, rather than symbolically.

Ivan and Jean now believe that the boy who drowned on the lake behind their house was intentionally drowned by his mother's boyfriend, and he came back to tell Ivan's family what had truly happened, using a clever variety of ways to get the attention of each person. If they are right, it certainly explains a lot.

Haunted Cemeteries
of Northern New York

Photo by Chris Sharlow
Apparition of a woman cradling a baby behind a gravestone in upper left corner of photograph?

Fear, respect, dread, comfort, curiosity, peace, and closure—few places on earth evoke as many intense mixed emotions as graveyards.

By day, we find solace in visiting the final resting places of our loved ones, hoping they are somehow watching over us, hearing our thoughts, seeing the tears we shed for them and how lovingly we plant flowers on their graves and pat the names that are etched into their stones; knowing how sad we are that they are gone, how much we miss them, how much we still wanted to say; and hoping that they can hear it now.

By night, we find our own paranoia and imagination working overtime as we quickly pass by the same cemetery, this time with our senses on full alert, half expecting to hear an eerie moan or see a moving shadow. Maybe we've watched too many horror movies or read too many scary books like this one, but cemeteries do that to us, contradictory as they are by nature.

On the one hand, we want to believe that the spirits of our loved ones are with us whenever we visit their graves; on the other, we're filled with fear at the thought of actually encountering a spirit we don't know in a cemetery—or even one we do know. The fact is, many people visit graveyards, silently speaking to loved ones who have died. But if you go there hoping to summon up spirits and see some excitement, and you put out a call to anyone who will listen, you may get more than you bargained for. Opportunistic and immoral souls can be found in any crowd, and it's no different in a graveyard where the souls happen to belong to the deceased—both the good and the bad.

Many people in Northern New York have experienced something unexplained in local graveyards, from the Brasher man who stumbled upon a decrepit hidden burial ground on an abandoned farm to a couple of guys who have really gotten up close and personal—one a gravedigger, the other, a spirit photographer. Their life-altering experiences, along with several convincing photographs, should serve as a reminder to always approach cemeteries with the deference and respect they deserve.

Mahoney Road, Brasher

It's the stuff of nightmares. A young man is walking through a barren field when he is roughly picked up by an unseen force and thrown into a nearby ditch. To add insult to injury, his car keys are ripped from his pocket and slapped across his face. What did he do to deserve such a rude welcoming? Apparently, he ventured too close to a burial ground that now lies in ruins.

It happened near an abandoned farm on the Mahoney Road in Brasher. The field he was in has a small remote cemetery where many, if not all, of the gravestones have toppled and are scattered about the land. The site is barely visible from the road.

The unfortunate victim refuses to ever go back near the property again.

Cemetery Caretaker, Massena

John Michaud III worked part-time for two years as a caretaker and gravedigger at cemeteries around Massena. His was a daunting task, saying goodbye to people he knew as he packed down the freshly turned soil over their graves, working diligently to maintain cemetery grounds . . . and, of course, dealing with the occasional ghostly apparition. In his words, he describes the two encounters that turned the self-ascribed skeptic into a firm believer.

"The first occurred during the summer of 1998. A man was working with me at the cemetery to fulfill his required probationary community service hours. The boss sent him off to push-mow in the old section of the cemetery. Within minutes he returned, frightened, and complained that he saw someone dressed in a dark suit who grinned at him, then suddenly disappeared before his eyes. He begged to be put anywhere but back over in that section. The boss and I chuckled, and the man was sent to another section of the cemetery.

"Some time later, I was cutting shrubbery in the cemetery when I noticed that a car had quietly driven around another caretaker's pick-up truck. While crouching over cutting a shrub, I noticed an older woman in a dress with pearls walking toward me. I assumed she was going to ask me the location of a buried relative and continued about my work, until her expected inquiry. It never came.

"When I looked up again, the woman had turned toward a gravestone and started to fade. She then completely disappeared, after floating right through the gravestone. I shook my head in disbelief. The other caretaker saw me and asked what was wrong. I quickly informed him that it was time to go for lunch!"

Spirit Photographer, Massena

Chris Sharlow is a spirit photographer who has spent the past few years researching Massena's oldest and most haunted cemeteries. He has taken hundreds of incredible photographs of ghosts in broad daylight, such as those shown below. While he has a gift for capturing apparitions on film, a gift can be like a two-edged sword in that it can help and it can hinder. For that reason, he does not recommend this type of research for everyone. He believes that "ghosts can attach themselves to those who accept them and seek them out" in cemeteries, himself having had many instances of ghosts following him home and disrupting the lives of all in the household.

Photo courtesy of Chris Sharlow
Chris Sharlow, spirit photographer.

The most common experience he has while actually taking photographs in cemeteries is hearing the whispering of spirits, and it has become more profuse every time he visits particular graveyards. He also sometimes feels like an invisible energy is pushing him from behind as he leaves a cemetery. He gets the feeling of being constantly watched or followed and sees shadows out of the corners of his eyes, especially when he's alone. A psychic told Chris that the spirits are "going to be around you for the rest of your life, because you sought them out."

Many things have occurred to him outside of cemeteries as a result of having been in them. He often feels as if he is being followed at home and has actually felt unseen hands touch him. Towels that hang in the bathroom get mysteriously repositioned. Lights go on and off with no human assistance. Ceiling fans malfunction, and so on.

One recent encounter in a local cemetery nearly made him give up his unusual hobby for good. He and a friend were "ghost-hunting," each using different cameras. They both happened to snap a picture at the same time, and when they did, sparks flew out from their flashes in every direction. Then a white mist started to take shape next to Chris, and he literally felt the presence of someone leaning on him, almost as if it were pushing him away. Both men saw it. Thoroughly frightened, they quickly left the premises.

Living Next to a Cemetery

Did you ever wonder what it would be like to live next door to a cemetery? A woman who lived in a house across the road from a local cemetery believes that a woman and a small girl haunt her former home where several people have seen their ghosts in the hallway at different times. She believes they came from the adjacent cemetery, because there is no history of death within the house itself that she's aware of.

A home on the same side of the road as the cemetery, and directly in front of the oldest section, is repeatedly up for sale, according to those who live nearby. It has changed owners many times over the years and always seems to start out the same, with the new owners moving in and fixing the house up a little. Then they begin to leave their outdoor lights on all night, and in a few months, another "For Sale" sign goes up on the front lawn. In fact, there is a sign on the lawn at the time of this writing.

Maybe you, too, know of such a house, now that you think of it.

Photo by Chris Sharlow
Cubic orb hovers above broken gravestone.

Photo by Chris Sharlow
A form that appears to be a soldier takes shape in the mist behind the large tombstone.

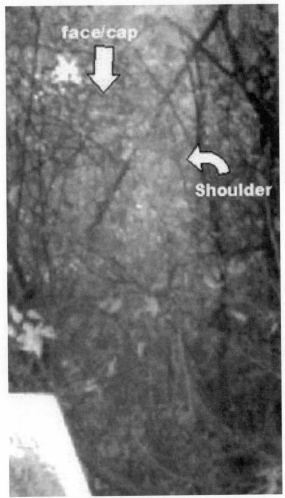

Soldier in the mist? An enlargement of the photo-graph on the previous page.

*Ominous face appears
in mist just above
brush line in upper left
corner.*
Photo by Chris Sharlow

*An enlargement of
the spirit face.*

The Others

Henderson, Black Lake, West Potsdam

There are more ghosts residing in Northern New York than you would believe, even if you were already a firm believer. While the majority of stories in this book are about ghosts that repeatedly reveal themselves to their witnesses in many different ways, it is far more common for people to experience one-time, isolated incidents. This type of experience can be so extraordinary as to convince us instantly that ghosts and spirits are certainly among us (or so subtle as to leave us questioning our own judgment and perception). I call them *The Others*—they are single, yet unforgettable, North Country encounters with the spirit world.

War or Eternal Unrest

A man who worked in the barn on his father's farm in Henderson took his life there in 1942, distraught over news of the war and his recent registration for selective service. The poor man would rather have spent an eternity working alone on his father's farm, than going off to war. And so it was.

Years later a young boy whose family had purchased the property often played around the abandoned barn, unaware of its tragic history. He recalls seeing, in broad daylight, the ghost of a man going about his usual business at work in the barn. Everything about the scene would have seemed entirely normal at the time, except that the man didn't belong there and that he was clearly a ghost—a ghost who seemed as surprised to see the boy as the boy was to see him.

The boy—as a grown man—was able to correctly choose the dead man from an old photo, without ever having seen his picture before.

Leave or You'll Lose Your Job

A woman who lived on Black Lake had an unfortunate run-in with a miserable homeowner—many years after he died. She was in her bedroom when the closet door opened. The spirit of the man who built the house appeared and told her the house was his, not hers. Furthermore, if she didn't leave, he would make sure she lost her new job in Ogdensburg. Three weeks later, she was indeed fired. Was it a self-fulfilling prophecy or the work of a vengeful spirit?

Saying Goodbye

It had been a nerve-racking day, but all was well that ended well. At least, Kim thought it had ended well, because the doctor told the family that her father "just had pneumonia." Assured that he would be fine in the hospital, Kim headed for home in West Potsdam and fell asleep around midnight.

About one o'clock, something woke her up. Her attention was drawn to the other side of the room where a misty form was taking shape and heading straight toward her. Just then, the phone rang, but she was too frightened by what she was witnessing to move. Her husband yelled for her to get the phone, which was on her side of the bed, effectively startling her out of her frozen trance-like state. When she finally managed to pick it up, she instinctively blurted out to whoever might be calling that she had just seen a ghost. Then she heard her aunt's voice, telling her to go to the hospital right away, because her father had taken a turn for the worse.

When Kim got to the hospital, she was told that they had nearly lost her father. She stayed with him that day, and he told her of his classic "near-death experience." He felt himself floating, there was no more pain, and he felt so good until he heard his name called, and then all the pain came back as they revived him.

Kim believes the ghost that came to her that night was either her father, to say goodbye when he was near death and briefly in a spirit form, or another spirit who was letting her know her father was in trouble. Either way, she said she and her father are no longer afraid of dying, because they now "know for sure there's more to this life than just what we see here."

Well said.

There's more to this life than just what we see here.

Sources

Courier and Freeman, March 25, 1901.

Evert's *History of St. Lawrence County,* 1878.

The Journal, August 30, 1973.

The Massena Observer, January 26, 1953; July 10, 1975.

The Post-Standard, August 20, 1930.

St. Lawrence County Historical Association Quarterly, Spring 1994.

Syracuse Herald, date unknown (early).

Watertown Daily Times, October 31, 1999.

Photograph Credits

Chris Sharlow of Massena, New York, took the photographs in the chapter called "Haunted Cemeteries." To order matted copies of Chris's amazing photographs, or to learn more about his large collection of spirit photography, you may leave a message at (315) 769-7063.

Ron Guindon of Toronto, Ontario, and his team of psychic investigators from around the North Country provided the photographs related to the investigation of "Spanky's Diner."

Gerina Dunwich provided the photographs of herself and the attic window in "Double, Double, Toil & Trouble."

Diane Murphy provided the photograph of the house in "Too Hot to Handle."

The photograph in "A Father & Daughter's Story" was provided by the anonymous daughter of that story.

All other photographs were taken by the author.

Cheri Revai is a North Country native who enjoys the local history and legends associated with this region. Last year she combined those interests with her love of research and writing to produce her first book, *Haunted Northern New York*.

She holds a degree in Secretarial Science from SUNY's Canton College of Technology and has been a secretary for seventeen years. She and her husband have four beautiful daughters from toddler to teen. They live in Northern New York.

She is currently collecting stories for a sequel to *Haunted Northern New York*, as well as working on a photo book with spirit photographer Chris Sharlow, *Gallery of North Country Ghosts*.